SPECIAL PRAISE FOR
BREAKING THE TRANCE

"Take heart, parents! It's not too late. Read this book. As an expert in the field of Internet addiction, I was delighted with this book and found the material fresh and practical. It will help parents as they try to cope with child rearing in the digital age."

Hilarie Cash, PhD, LMHC, Founding Member, Chief Clinical Officer, and Education Director for reSTART Life

• • •

"If you are a parent, grandparent, or anyone who cares about kids and their ability to become responsible, happy adults at some point, you should care about the valuable information in this book. The authors' balance real-life case stories, research, and common sense about how to tackle the monster that has crept into every family and relationship— that tantalizing screen—and provide explanations and simple tools that are both encouraging and empowering to move from identification to action. In addition, there is enough information and guidance in this book to help schools work effectively in tandem with the families they serve to help young people (and their parents) find specific ways to connect, grow stronger, and develop the skills necessary to lead fulfilling, meaningful lives."

Jackie Booth, PhD, Parent, grandparent, and lifelong educator

BREAKING THE TRANCE

BREAKING
THE
TRANCE

A PRACTICAL GUIDE FOR PARENTING
THE SCREEN-DEPENDENT CHILD

GEORGE T. LYNN

WITH CYNTHIA C. JOHNSON

CENTRAL RECOVERY PRESS

LAS VEGAS

Central Recovery Press (CRP) is committed to publishing exceptional materials addressing addiction treatment, recovery, and behavioral healthcare topics.

For more information, visit www.centralrecoverypress.com.

Publisher: Central Recovery Press
 3321 N. Buffalo Drive
 Las Vegas, NV 89129

21 20 19 18 17 16 1 2 3 4 5

Library of Congress Cataloging-in-Publication Data

Names: Lynn, George T., 1945- author. | Johnson, Cynthia C., 1959- author.
Title: Breaking the trance : a practical guide for parenting the screen-dependent child / George T. Lynn, with Cynthia C. Johnson.
Description: Las Vegas : Central Recovery Press, [2016] | Includes bibliographical references.
Identifiers: LCCN 2016024213 (print) | LCCN 2016036428 (ebook) | ISBN 9781942094265 (alk. paper) | ISBN 9781942094272
Subjects: LCSH: Video games and children. | Video game addiction. | Parenting.
Classification: LCC HQ784.V53 L96 2016 (print) | LCC HQ784.V53 (ebook) | DDC 794.8083--dc23
LC record available at https://lccn.loc.gov/2016024213

Photo of George T. Lynn by Vakker Portraits. Used with permission.
Photo of Cynthia C. Johnson by Heidi Winklepleck. Used with permission.

Every attempt has been made to contact copyright holders. If copyright holders have not been properly acknowledged, please contact us. Central Recovery Press will be happy to rectify the omission in future printings of this book.

Publisher's Note: This book contains general information about child development, screen dependence, and related matters. The information is not medical advice. This book is not an alternative to medical advice from your doctor or other professional healthcare provider.

Our books represent the experiences and opinions of their authors only. Every effort has been made to ensure that events, institutions, and statistics presented in our books as facts are accurate and up-to-date. To protect their privacy, the names of some of the people, places, and institutions in this book may have been changed.

Cover design by The Book Designers.
Interior design and layout by Sara Streifel, Think Creative Design

To my children, Andrea, Renetta, Chloe, Dane, and Morgan, the brilliant spirits, creative minds, and loves of my life! Thank you for being my children and teaching me!

Cynthia

To my mother, Margaret Mary Lynn, who gifted me with the example of her bravery, compassion, and authenticity.

George

TABLE OF CONTENTS

ACKNOWLEDGMENTS

We first want to acknowledge our clients. Wow! Such marvelous children and incredible parents who have let us see their lives and hold their stories. We are honored to be accepted as their consultants and allies. All of them are dealing with so much more than we dealt with growing up. The world is so different now, so much more confusing, holding both more promise and more risk. They have let us see who they are in their day-to-day struggle to be real in a world infused with the sparkling and entrancing wonders of screen media.

After our clients, we thank our colleagues who also assist the families we serve, especially Dr. Hilarie Cash and Cosette Rae, MSW, pioneering founders of reSTART Life, LLC—the first rehabilitation center in the United States for young adults afflicted with serious screen dependence—who have provided their insight and let us feature the screening tool they use in their intake process (the BIGS-P).

We also want to thank the good folks at Waterside Productions, especially Senior Literary Agent Margot Hutchison, for helping us bring this book to the attention of parents who hopefully will benefit from its perspective and the strategies it provides. And our thanks to our publisher, Central Recovery Press, especially to Janet Ottenweller, our editor.

A final thank you goes out to our readers for giving us the opportunity to share some of the things we have learned watching families who have made it through the confusing maze of wired, modern life to bring the children they love back to their senses and back to the important priorities of being successful at school and in their relationships with their peers and parents.

From George

First, there is Thom Hartmann, whom I have known from his days as sysop of the CompuServe ADHD Forum (around the time my first book on ADD came out). I cannot thank Thom enough for taking an interest in my work and helping me get my voice out into the world. I have learned from his passion and drive what it takes to make a difference.

I would also like to acknowledge several of my intellectual mentors in the art of "being real": psychiatrist Dr. Erich Fromm, philosopher Dr. Jean Houston, mythologist Michael Meade, and master psychotherapist Dr. Erving Polster. Erving used to say, "Follow your excitement. Follow your clients' excitement, and you can't go wrong." Erving and the others have provided me with the example of their lives, grounded in deep and honest interest in people, and in humility, humor, and gracious compassion. Following their own excitement, they have taught me so much.

From Cynthia

First, there are my daughters, Chloe Goldbloom, graphic artist extraordinaire who did the illustrations for this book, and Andrea Goldbloom, Facebook and website aficionado for the book. I appreciate their incredible hard work, support, and inspiration. And there are my brilliant and caring siblings, Steve Johnson and Christine Johnson. No one could have asked for a more loving brother and sister. Their encouragement and counsel are both heartfelt. Thank you.

And I thank my colleague and mentor, John McKinnon, self-described "Evangelist of Fitness," an absolute master at the art of physical healing and wellness who provided his observations of what is happening to the bodies of so many kids today as a result of recreational screen dependence.

Finally, there is my brilliant mom, the late Jeanne Johnson. My love of learning and teaching are greatly informed by her presence in my life.

INTRODUCTION

Why Taking Charge Is Easier Said Than Done

If you are the parent of a child who has an unhealthy relationship with his cell phone, video games, and other screen media, you are in the company of millions of parents who feel confused and out of control when it comes to managing their children's screen media use.

This book has been written for the parents of children who *used* to be seen on playgrounds. Go to your nearest city park or public playground. With the exception of mothers with very young children, you will not see many kids of elementary or middle school age. No boys and girls hanging out, teasing and chasing each other or doing kid things. None of that. The older children who happen to be there are probably sitting on a bench, heads bowed over their cell phones. Even outside on the grass and in the sun, life is virtual.

I am a psychotherapist who has written books on parenting children with neuropsychiatric challenges such as **attention-deficit/ hyperactivity disorder (ADHD), Asperger's syndrome,** and **bipolar disorder.** My coauthor, Cynthia Johnson, is an educator. We are both parents.

When I first went into practice as a psychotherapist thirty years ago, I worked with families in distress as well as adults and children individually. My training in family dynamics and counseling psychology served me well. Children came to my practice motivated to work on some torment in their lives, some suffering. I was chosen to hear their stories about a particular issue and help them get some resolution.

I almost never see this sort of presenting issue in my practice now. Fully 80 percent of the children, teens, and young adults I serve now have some problem that is directly or indirectly a result of **screen dependence.** Usually the child is failing at school and blaming everything and everyone else for his failure without ever mentioning the fact that he only gets four hours of sleep each night. It may take several meetings for it to become clear that the anxiety disorder or depression a child is experiencing is a direct result of a screen dependency, because children with screen dependence tend to be clever at not mentioning the issue.

Concurrently, Cynthia was running into more children in her tutoring work whose lives were plagued by screen dependence. She suggested we write this book to highlight the scope and severity of the issue and to provide practical strategies to deal with it because we were hearing and seeing a pattern in what the parents whose families we serve had to say.

- "It is so confusing. How can we put limits on something that makes our child so obviously happy? Maybe there are educational benefits: his hand-eye coordination may improve, and perhaps his ability to think quickly will help him on his driver's exam."

- "Yes, his grades are declining, and he tells us he does not care about school, or that it is boring, and he is smarter than his teachers. But his grades don't reflect that explanation."

- "Yes, most of the friends he had before he got into gaming are either gamers or gone in his life. He really doesn't seem to have any social confidence or ability to decide things for himself. He seems very immature in these regards for his age. And yes, we are concerned about his physical health and development. His sleeping habits are horrible, and all he eats is junk food. He doesn't move much and he just looks physically weak!"

- "Oh yes, he is also very manipulative and will do anything to avoid homework, studying, or any kind of hard work, but you know, that's just the way kids are. They lie to you."

At this point, Cynthia or I might inquire of the parents, "So, if you are seeing a variety of detrimental effects as a result of his screen media use, why don't you put a stop to it? After all, you're in charge."

Many parents answer this query with the following response: "It may seem that we are in control, but we are not. First, we do not have the time to ride herd on him all the time. Second, he needs to be more responsible. Third, he is trying, really. Fourth, all his friends are gamers or spend a lot of time with YouTube and **social media.** We have very little control over what he does at their homes. And finally, we would do something if we could, but what can we do? We cannot go back to the nineteenth century."

We cannot go backward in time and make digital media go away, but ironically, in allowing our children unlimited access to it, we *are* seeing them regress intellectually, emotionally, and morally—a bold statement. In the chapters that follow, we will provide data to back up our assertions, as well as ways for you to assess and measure screen media use practices in your family. We will show you how to implement a screen control plan based on your own definition of your family's values that works and is enforceable. And we will provide specific and practical ways to assess the degree of your child's screen media use problem and take action to correct it.

The importance of parental trance-formation

It is commonly believed that children abuse screen media because parents are absent. To some extent this is true, but it is important to point out that parents have always had to be absent for one reason or another: one parent, or both, was in the military; career demands required a lot of away-from-home travel; or a parent had to leave to work one or several jobs to make ends meet.

All of this being true, it is imperative to note that it is the screen media and the indoctrination everyone has had in the inevitability of its influence in our lives that make this a problem greater than absent parenting. In fact, many parents spend as much time using recreational screen media as their children do. So we need to look deeper at the problem of why many parents ignore the toxic influence of screen media in their lives as well as their children's lives.

We do not agree with the pervasive inevitability of screen media taking control. You are in charge. You can take back control. It can be done. You can do things as parents that bring your children back into physical contact with siblings, friends, and others who love them. You can help them remedy their miserable academic achievement so they begin to have intellectual confidence. But you are going to have to get out of the parental **trance state** you are in to help your children.[1]

Your personal beliefs about what it means to be a good parent shape the way you see things. You, I, all of us tend to see things as *we* are, not as *they* are. Imagine all of us moving through our lives surrounded by an invisible bubble made up of messages, all our beliefs and expectations. We do not really see the world objectively but always interpret it through the messages written on that invisible bubble, as if in a **trance**. As a parent, your parental trance state is made up of what your parents taught you, as well as the decisions you made growing up about your parents and how they treated you. You may have the following beliefs:

- "I, myself (the parent), am on my screen media at work every fifteen minutes or so, all day long. There's really nothing wrong with that—it's just the way things are these days."

- "The best parents are best friends with their children. If my children do not like me, it is my fault!"

- "My kids trust me, and I trust them. Why should I track their screen media use? That is a violation of the way we are as a family."

- "If my child does not want to do something, there is no way I can make him do it."

- "If I am too strict, I will traumatize him and alienate him from me for life."

- "It is my job to protect him from pain and make things easier for him in his life."

- "There is no way I will ever understand all the technology. I just need to make sure he has every advantage by getting him the stuff that my friends (other parents) get for their children."

- "The worst thing for my child's social reputation is for us to look like the weirdos on the block—the only family who doesn't use a lot of digital media."

There is an adage from psychotherapeutic practice used in the treatment of war veterans suffering from post-traumatic stress disorder: "We do the best we can given the information we have at the time." This pithy statement has been used to nurture self-acceptance for thousands of veterans who blame themselves for things they did in a war.

So, speaking directly now, parent to parent, we urge you to forgive yourself for not knowing what to do when it comes to your children's screen usage! We are all in this together. We are all making the best decisions we can based on the information we have.

As mentioned earlier, you are in charge; however, there is a second part to that statement: you are in charge, but you don't know it! In fact, just as digital media have entranced your son or daughter with some particular form of screen delight, you are entranced within your idea of what it means to be a good parent, and that trance is held in place by all the beliefs you have about worthiness that you learned from your parents and society.

A fish does not know it is breathing water. As modern parents, it is difficult to understand how the digital medium that we "swim" in has taken hold and shaped our expectations and beliefs about what a good parent is.

Many parents feel like hypocrites when it comes to putting tighter screen controls on their children. In the morning, the first thing they do is look at their cell phones to determine their priorities for the next few hours. Then they check their phones again. And again. And when returning from work or school, the first thing most parents do is go to their computers, not to each other.

If you are going to have a positive effect in your children's lives, the trance state circumscribed with the beliefs noted above needs to be replaced with *another* trance state that gives you a new range of options:

- "I am a parent. I am in charge. I do the best I can and put the rest in my personal 'God Box,' a symbolic container that holds things I would like to change but cannot change without God's help."

- "I cannot spare my child his trouble (the consequences of his behavior) or his suffering—the pain he experiences from boredom, isolation, or frustration. His troubles become his teacher. I have no right to deprive him of it."

- "If I die tomorrow, I want him to remember me as a person who put my relationships with *people* first. I do not want to be remembered as an isolated person who only had online friends. I want him to see me having healthy relationships with real people, which are messy at times."

- "I am not a victim of the Internet. My child is not a victim of incompetent schooling. No victims here. I face life and teach him to face life in terms of challenge, not in terms of curse or blessing."

- "*Strict* parenting can definitely be *loving* parenting. If I have to have tighter oversight in my home, I accept that responsibility. Someone's got to do it. I can't be a nice guy all the time."

When you start living these values, changing your child's behavior at home and school becomes *what you do*. And it is actually not that difficult to turn things around once you are committed. Here is what we have observed in families led by parents who have successfully implemented screen controls in their homes.

- People actually talk *with* each other about important things. They come from the heart and are honest.

- Children may not like all of school, but they value some of it and continue to *study* and do homework. They understand that their primary job is to develop themselves intellectually. This may not be easy, but that is what they do.

- Family members enjoy each other's company. They laugh together, eat together, play together, work together, and occasionally argue passionately with each other about things that are important.

- There is a sense of vibrancy, sassiness, and connection in the home. You can feel the spirit when walking in the door.

How often do you experience this kind of emotional contact in your own household? If you do not get enough of this kind of energy, consider making some changes in how people prioritize their time in your home. Give it a try. Jump out of your comfort zone as your child's best friend and create a new zone for both of you in which you assume responsibility for stewardship of his potential.

Why screen dependent instead of addicted?

In the news, we hear a lot about children who are "addicted" to recreational screen media and the Internet. Addicts are typically people who have a physical, mental, emotional, and spiritual reaction to the use of mind- or mood-altering chemicals or certain behaviors. They do not think it through and behave compulsively and impulsively. Addicts protect their impulsive behavior with lies, excuses, and manipulation, and their substance use or practice "creates a significant barrier to achieving ordinary life goals." A person with an **addiction** has one priority in life—satisfying that addiction.[2]

In terms of psychological dynamics, research shows that addictive behavior is pushed by *shame*. The addict enacts his addictive practice or takes his addictive drug and feels ashamed, using it again to soothe his shame. This is where there is a big difference between shame-based addicts and children who are screen dependent. Typically the latter do not experience shame for excessive screen media use because society has not assigned the label of "shameful" to this practice. The absence of shame or guilt and the presence of personal pride in the degree of overuse create the necessity for finding a term other than *addiction* to describe obsessive use of digital media.[3]

Rather than the term *addicted,* the preferred term is *screen dependent* (SD). By this we mean the child or young adult is accessing more than an hour a day of recreational screen media (this does not include using digital media for homework), and he is only marginally interested in anything other than his screen avocations. The degree of screen dependence can be measured by the degree of difficulty the child has at home and school achieving ordinary life goals as well as the degree of regression in the social, emotional, and cognitive domains of his personality.

Screen dependent is a more appropriate term because children who use recreational screen media can be grouped, using a range of dependence from mild to severe. This cannot be done if addiction terminology is used. You are either an addict or you are not. In our client research we find many variations, so the use of *screen dependent* as a term makes more sense.

Our client research suggests that most children do not experience the severity of psychological dependence that those with true addictive states experience. Yes, the child may be flunking all his classes at school or be miserably depressed and anxious, unsure of who he is and totally unable to organize himself toward any goal, but he is not drooling, shaking, passing out in a pool of vomit, or getting arrested. He is most likely not stealing to fund his screen dependence. He is not living on the streets; he is not driving in his car under the influence. He is just in his room with the lights turned low, the place where he goes unless he is required to be somewhere else.

So let's look at the range of severity for a moment. At the least extreme of the range, we see children tethered to their cell phones and texting, but they can put the devices away at night and get a good night's sleep. And they have other interests, such as the robotics club, soccer, tennis, lacrosse, swimming, music, or church activities.

At the greatest extreme of the range, there are the children who have manipulated their parents into submission and use recreational screen media more than eleven hours a day. These children tend to show a physical growth pattern that lags in developmental milestones. They are vulnerable to the development of neurological issues evocative of a severe case of ADHD, anxiety disorder, or pediatric bipolar disorder with its chronic and aggressive mood states.

Children with severe screen dependence may refuse to go to school and may carry failing grades in most of their classes. Their screen activities may border on the delusional—they make up props for their game play, such as using labeled colored water as a "power potent" to give them strength through some mythical combat adventure in their video games. Currently there is no research that looks at correlations between chronic recreational screen media use and severe dependence and the development of psychosis, but the analysis of my adolescent client population suggests that a very powerful *unipolar depression,* which does not have the bipolar highs, can result from severe screen dependence and the sleep deprivation attendant to that dependence.

In terms of measurement of severity, we set the norm of our continuum based on current research that suggests that, on the average, American children in the eight-to-ten-year-old range use screen media of all kinds *nearly eight hours a day,* with older children typically logging *eleven hours a day.* This includes television, but the time spent watching television is gradually being overtaken by media on cell phones and tablets and, in a third to a half of households, children are now accessing television on their cell phones, iPods, and computers. On the average, children in all age groups split their recreational screen media time among social media, video viewing, gaming, and texting. Teenagers send an average of 3,364 text messages a month. They prefer texting to actual phone conversations and use the phone less than geriatric populations.[4]

Severity of Screen Dependence (hours per day of recreational screen media use)		
MILD 2 hours	MODERATE 8 hours	SEVERE 14 hours

Our clinical research confirms that children in grades K–12 spend more time using recreational and social media than most people imagine. The Severity of Screen Dependence continuum gives a capsule view of the amount of time children use screen media. The numbers of children and adolescents who make up the eight-hour average of the screen-dependent population cluster on each side of the moderate range. In terms of hours online, the numbers suggest that about half of the studied population spend eight hours or less on recreational screen media and half spend eight hours or more. We believe that children in the middle of the "mild" to "moderate" range are most at risk. These children are compulsive users who fly under the radar. They are greatly at risk because they can hide their dependence for years and, in their devotion to it, not really take on any serious goals or challenges in their lives. They are secluded in their virtual worlds and avoid all the stress, trials, errors, and other learning experiences that move a child through his or her development to adulthood.

Recommendations of the American Academy of Pediatrics for safe daily recreational screen media use

In 2013, the American Academy of Pediatrics (**AAP**) released their revised recommendations for pediatricians to guide their patient-parents in home management of recreational screen media.[5] These recommendations call for

- limiting all recreational screen media use to less than two hours each day, with less than one hour per day being an optimal choice;

- disallowing screen media use altogether for children under the age of two;

- keeping televisions, computers, and interconnected digital devices out of children's bedrooms;

- monitoring closely children's online use, including social media sites;

- coviewing recreational and educational programs to promote discussion of family values concerning screen media use;

- establishing household screen controls, including rules for use of all recreational screen media, social media, and texting, along with enforcement of nightly media curfews.

The AAP suggests that pediatricians ask two questions of parents, which frame the structure of the book:

1. How many hours a day does your child spend using screen media?

2. Does he have digital media devices in his room?

In Chapter 1, we discuss using a **Screen Media Use Recording Form.** This provides a simple way to assess the number of hours your child is involved with recreational screen media. In Chapter 11, we provide guidelines for making sure bedrooms are device-free by a scheduled time each day.

Other research supports the AAP safe use standard of two hours per day or less, stating that no measureable neurologic changes occur at this level, which suggests that when the child hits three hours or more of recreational screen media use each day, destructive changes in brain function (involving mood issues, mental processing, and organization) begin to occur.[6]

By and large, the recommendations we provide in this book include all the **AAP guidelines** along with a description of specific methods for implementing these recommendations.

Getting a decent grade point average is *not* the most important reason for screen controls

When looking carefully at the screen-dependent child population, we find many children are actually doing okay academically. Although they may not be working to potential, why should parents be concerned about their children's screen media use if they are earning Bs and Cs? After all, their ability to move through the grades shows that they can focus on other things. What's the big deal?

A child's nervous system needs to be put in situations in which he has to use his mind and talents to overcome *real*, not *virtual*, obstacles. This process begins with boredom. Deprived of access to recreational screen media, the child becomes bored and deals with the boredom by finding things to do. The child's brain needs this type of boredom because without it, it cannot exercise neurons that are part of the imagining process. This is how all of us develop the skills and wisdom to grow up—by imagining our lives and finding resourceful ways to bring that imagination into reality.

Curiosity is the first step. The child is struck by what is different about something and drawn toward it to find out. He begins to learn how to differentiate patterns, which requires a bit of solitude. But more importantly, this process begins *within* the child, when his mind is ready for it.

The video game industry would have consumers believe that it can sell applications that can make this process start *outside* the child and help his imagination produce results given the correct cue, resulting in learning. However, the research suggests that this does not happen. Contrary to millions of dollars' worth of game company propaganda, recreational screen media use *does not* make child users more creative, any more than applications like *Baby Einstein* improve the vocabulary of toddlers.[7] Yes, a game gives the player problems to solve, but these problems have nothing to do with reality. Solving a particular problem involves becoming better at following a set of rules that structure the game play. Video games do not improve critical thought or creative thinking. They simply require that the child become good at anticipating the will and godlike presence of the game's designers.

As stated earlier, many of the children who occupy the middle of the recreational screen media use continuum, the "normal majority," get okay grades. But this does not insulate these children from the destructive impact of screen dependence any more than children who have more severe school-adjustment issues. Getting passable grades at school should not be a ticket to screen media use nirvana. Although grade-point average (GPA) figures importantly into parents' assessment of the presence of screen dependence, getting a decent GPA cannot be the sole criterion for success. Returning to life—to the messy world of social relationships outside the child's bedroom—or perhaps to a job, an art, or an avocation is a vastly more important end point than simply turning in homework that was dashed out in a half hour in order to return to screen media for another five hours.

We are not demonizing digital media

Before we continue further, we would like to make this statement clear: We are not against the use of digital media. With some exceptions, we do not consider the invention and promulgation of screen media to be a social disease or (in most cases) a dark and deceitful business. It is simply a business, a way of making money. We do not condemn technology; rather, *we caution about the damage overuse of certain technology does to the minds of growing children.*

There are many settings in which screen media and video games provide a powerful *assist* to government and society. Virtualization is used in a variety of specialized educational settings, such as training programs for architectural and engineering design. Using virtual technology readily available today, anyone can attend a class by sitting in a virtual room with other **avatar** students taking the same subject from an avatar instructor and earn college credit. The beauty of virtual design lies in its ability to simulate potential situations clearly and in such detail that people can be thoroughly trained in a particular task before actually dealing with it in real life.[8]

Also, there are a variety of medical applications of screen media currently under development. The United States military, for example, is exploring the use of video games in medical procedures done with severely burned soldiers returning from Afghanistan. They have found that patients can tolerate the extreme pain involved in peeling off tissue that has been mortified by burns if they are allowed to play video games depicting snowball fights while having their dead flesh excoriated.[9] The fact that screen media can greatly ameliorate the experience of extreme pain testifies to the power of game technology to go deep enough into the human nervous system to effect autonomic reactions, as well as reduce ordinary psychological stress.[10]

Another positive use of gaming technology includes systems designed to help autistic youngsters learn social behavior behind avatars they build for themselves and run with others in a virtual environment.[11] The sky is the limit in terms of the potential good that can come from more sophisticated virtualization applications.

The structure of the book

There are several good books in print on the topic of screen overuse by children and adults in modern society. But our survey did not find books that describe a process for writing a **screen control plan** that was something other than a variation on the parental lecture method. Therefore, we wanted to give readers a method they could use that had a good track record for getting buy-in from screen-dependent children and gave parents specific ways to handle issues on a day-to-day basis.

- Chapter 1 describes ways to assess a child's screen media use to determine if he has a screen dependency.

- Chapters 2 through 9 provide information on the dynamics we see in modern families that maintain the *status quo* and resist corrective action, even in the face of strong evidence that more control on screen media use is needed.

- Chapters 10 and 11 describe a two-phased process for dealing with the screen media use issue. Chapter 10 details how to develop a statement of family values and the **behavior standards** that flow from these values. Chapter 11 describes the mechanics of writing a screen control plan and the various ways it can be enforced, including use of a **level system.**

- Chapter 12 provides pointers for helping a formerly screen-dependent child recover and shows how to build family practices that are sustainable.

These chapters, taken together, form the knowledge base for implementing a home screen control plan.

Use of masculine pronouns

Throughout the book, masculine pronouns are used to make the text more reader-friendly. We do not deny that screen dependence is a significant problem for girls—who sustain damage in overuse of social media more than gaming—but our research does suggest that more boys are screen dependent, and they are more aggressive in their dependence than girls. When we do come across a situation that could as easily apply to a girl as it could to a boy, feminine pronouns will be used.

HOW TO IMPLEMENT A HOUSEHOLD SCREEN CONTROL PLAN

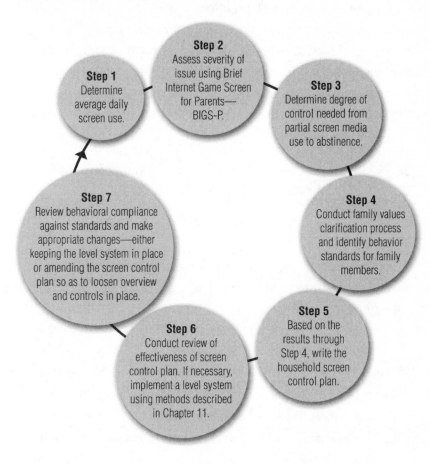

Step 1
Determine average daily screen use.

Step 2
Assess severity of issue using Brief Internet Game Screen for Parents—BIGS-P.

Step 3
Determine degree of control needed from partial screen media use to abstinence.

Step 4
Conduct family values clarification process and identify behavior standards for family members.

Step 5
Based on the results through Step 4, write the household screen control plan.

Step 6
Conduct review of effectiveness of screen control plan. If necessary, implement a level system using methods described in Chapter 11.

Step 7
Review behavioral compliance against standards and make appropriate changes—either keeping the level system in place or amending the screen control plan so as to loosen overview and controls in place.

A note about families

Please understand our inference that all families have a mother and father living together with a child or children. Single parents manage a third of households in the United States, with a high preponderance of those parents being single moms.[12] The stress on single parents is enormous, and we do not want to suggest otherwise. This being said, we believe the method we suggest works for single-parent homes as well as it does for two-parent households.

We, the authors, are both parents. I am the father of three grown children, and Cynthia is the mother of five. We know that it is easy to promote strong family practices but much more difficult to implement these practices. We have great respect for all the families we have worked with who are wrestling with the problem of their children's screen media use, as well as the problem of trying to make a living in our complex and demanding economic environment. We approach you, our parent readers, as fellow travelers on this road.

The Tree Trance Story

by Cynthia

Everyone has some kind of trance story . . . a seemingly subtle situation right in front of your eyes that you are unaware of until it becomes "Oh! I get it now!" obvious. The following is my tree trance story.

I was raised on an eye-popping 640-acre farm in southern Oregon. My grandparents lived on the original early 1900s homestead located on the lower portion of the property. The fields around their home were alive with swaying corn and flowers, grazing cows, and herds of meandering wild elk. As a child I would run through the rows of gigantic corn with my arms stretched out wide and listen to the slap-slap-slap sound on my wrists. My immediate family lived on "the ranch," a modern home built on a hill with a 180-degree *unobstructed* view overlooking my grandparents' farmhouse.

Fast-forward many decades. My sister, Christine, and I were tasked with selling the ranch after our parents passed. When Christine informed me that the intended buyers were concerned about the trees obstructing the view, I was completely confused and flabbergasted. "What trees? There are no trees! The view is spectacular!" We decided to meet on the property and see for ourselves what the real situation was regarding the trees. After the initial hugs, my sister and I walked over to the tree trouble area.

I still was talking about "What trees? What obstructed view?" when Christine took my hand and placed it on one of the fifty-foot trees *right in from of me!* I was stunned; I had not seen it.

Not one, not two, but five huge trees now were growing on the property. Naturally, I had no memory of them because they were planted after we left. But my eyes were in a trance, clouded by memory, until I physically touched the trees. Talk about not seeing the forest through the trees!

• • •

Are there areas of your life as a parent where you are in a trance? For example, do you gloss over the amount of time your children are using recreational screen media? When a thought comes to your mind about your child being in his room alone for hours playing video games, watching YouTube, or using his smartphone, do you dismiss it as silly worry and perhaps remain in a trance? Have any other parents meandered down the trail of trance and mentioned that they have concerns about what gaming is doing to one of their children? Does that move you?

Likewise, is your daughter or son in her or his own trance? Does either of them change the subject or try to reassure you when nonacademic screen time is mentioned? Does either of them get angry or frustrated if screen time is limited? Do you see personality changes that disturb you?

And, most importantly, would your children limit screen time on their own if it were damaging them? Are they strong or mature enough to make that choice for themselves?

I suggest you ask yourself, as a parent, what your *bottom line* is. How bad does it have to get before you see how chronic screen dependence has changed your child's personality, emotional life, academic capability, and overall physical well-being? We all do the best we can given the information we have. I needed my sister to put my hand on one of those big trees to get my wake-up call.

Listening to my clients, I observe that the parents who finally "see" the screen-dependence trance understand that *they* are in charge and *can* make the necessary changes to help their children have an unobstructed view of life, thus reaching their full potential. As these parents remember that they are in charge, the trance lifts.

In fact, let me suggest that when you start wavering in your determination to make positive changes in your family, as we suggest in this book, talk to yourself. In your inner speech, call yourself by name and remind yourself, "You are in charge!" This awareness reminder will feel like a supportive hand on your shoulder.

CHAPTER 1

How to Determine Whether Your Child Is Screen Dependent

By our definition, a child is screen dependent if she or he has a compulsive engagement with screen media use despite adverse consequences, such as failing in school or losing a face-to-face social network. How can you determine whether your child's use of screen media is sufficient to cross the threshold from being a *pastime* to being a *compulsion*? How do you know whether your child's use of screen media is *normal and nondestructive* or *destructive, chronic, and dependent*?

The first step: getting an accurate measure of the issue

Your decision to investigate whether your child has an issue with screen dependence should be guided by two things: you need to know how much time your child spends engaging in recreational screen media, and you need to analyze the type of media she or he accesses and the impacts of use, if any, on the child's success in life. A Screen Media Use Recording Form can be used to start the process.[13] Here is an example of how the form would show information for a middle schooler named Jake.

Screen Media Use Recording Form Jake Smith						
DAY/TIME	SCHOOL RELATED?	MEDIA	HARDWARE	DURATION IN HOURS	HOURS OF SLEEP PREVIOUS NIGHT	GPA / MISC.
3/7/16 4:00 p.m.	N	Minecraft	Xbox One	4	4	2.1
3/7/16 8:00 p.m.	N	Following Tumblr account	Phone	3	4	
3/7/16 to 3/8/16 Midnight to 2:00 a.m.	N	Snapchat	Phone	2	4	
3/8/16 Beginning at 7:30 a.m.	N	Texting	Phone	9	5	Quiz missed/ LA/SS

The information noted in the form helps parents track actual screen media use.

1. What was the day and time of the observation?

2. Is screen media use related to school? Write "Y" or "N" and note details.

3. Which screen media are being accessed? Note specific details (Instagram, YouTube, texting, video game, Twitter, Tumblr, Snapchat, etc.).

4. What type of hardware is the child is using: tablet, Internet phone, **game console,** desktop, or smartphone?

5. What is the estimated time using screen media (hours and minutes)?

6. What was the child's sleep duration the night prior to the observation?

7. What is the child's current GPA? Cite along with other school-related information.

Screen media use should be recorded for at least three weeks. Simultaneously, the child should be evaluated using the **Brief Internet Game Screen - For Parents (BIGS-P)** discussed in the next section.[14] A good baseline is important because it establishes the degree to which screen media use is contributing to a child's school performance problem. More than an hour a day of recreational screen media use begins to suggest that the child is willfully reprioritizing his time away from school toward screen media.

A poor GPA suggests the presence of a **learning disability (LD),** a personal organization issue, and/or an unwillingness to put effort into school, foregoing studying and homework for gaming and other screen pursuits. If a child is accessing recreational screen media for *less than an hour a day* and is having difficulty at school, investigation of his or her learning issues should occur using either a **504 Plan** or an **Individualized Education Plan (IEP).**

The 504 Plan is derived from Section 504 of the Rehabilitation Act.[15] It protects people with disabilities at work and in school by allowing modification of the work or classroom environment, such as where a student sits (to reduce distractibility) or whether she or he is allowed more time for test taking. This modification helps children who are anxious or slower processors, as is seen in attention-deficit/hyperactivity disorder (ADHD).[16]

Setting up an IEP for a child puts the child in **special education,** which may lead to a different placement in public or private school or provision of additional educational services, such as tutoring at the school district's expense. The IEP process begins with an assessment of the child's learning style by identifying learning disabilities or other issues that are interfering with school success. Excessive screen media use would not be considered a qualifying condition to set up an IEP.

Assessing your child's recreational screen dependence using the BIGS-P

Screen dependence can be measured from mild to moderate or severe. The BIGS-P is an instrument developed by the **reSTART Life** Center located outside Redmond, Washington.[17] The screening tool includes criteria seen in the proposed description for Internet Gaming Disorder in the *Diagnostic and Statistical Manual of Mental Disorders (**DSM-5**).*[18] (This classification will likely be included in the next edition of the *DSM*.) Each of the eleven questions on the BIGS-P asks for either a "yes" or "no" response or a specific rating. Once you have completed the questionnaire, located in Appendix 2, score the results using the table at the end of the questionnaire.

The BIGS-P is targeted toward assessment of *video game dependence* specifically, but it also provides a good measurement of dependence for other content-specific functions, such as viewing videos, using social media, and texting.

Our take on specific BIGS-P questions

Here we take a quick look at the questions on the BIGS-P, which we consider to be the "gold standard" for assessment of screen dependence. Please note that the section that follows does not include input from reSTART. Our interpretation of the meaning and importance of each question is just that—our interpretation.

1. **How often do you feel your son or daughter thinks about their current, previous, or next gaming activity?**
   This question gauges *preoccupation* with screen media use. Preoccupation is an issue when you always have the

feeling that even when your child talks about something not connected to screen media, *she or he can't wait to talk about that very thing.* Here we see the screen-dependent child losing interest in all the things and people that used to be interesting. The only thing that lights up her or his face is delight with some favorite screen medium. One way of testing for preoccupation is to ask your child, without reference to screen media, what activities she or he finds to be *most exciting.* If the first response you get relates to screen media, consider the possibility of a problem.

2. **Has your son or daughter become restless, irritable, angry, or anxious when unable to engage in gaming activities?** This question assesses for the presence of *withdrawal symptoms,* a core aspect of any neurological dependence, which the *DSM-5* describes as "irritability, anxiety, and sadness."[19] We see these features in screen-dependent children along with the presence of apathy and listlessness. The child feels lost without a screen media connection—lonely, friendless, and depressed.

3. **Has her/his engagement with gaming activities increased in the past year?** This question evaluates for the presence of *tolerance.* As the brain acclimates to one level of screen media use, in keeping with research about the neurobiology of dependence, it creates a demand for more use. Dependence becomes worse over time. The child requires greater involvement in screen media to stay in a good mood. As in the case of other dependencies, use increases to avoid withdrawal symptoms, but the pain-reduction effect decreases with each new use. This is similar to people with substance addictions—half of them use an addictive chemical to get high, and the other half use it to avoid the pain of withdrawal.

4. **What is the average number of hours your son or daughter spends engaging in gaming activities each week?** This question provides a measure of the *severity of tolerance.* As noted in the Introduction, less than an hour of recreational screen media use (all types) per day indicates the brain has not acclimated to increased use and the problem is under control. Screen media use between one and two hours per day starts pushing the nervous system to reset with a higher demand for use. Some issues with personal organization and fatigue may become evident. Once tolerance builds to the point where the child requires more than two hours of use per day, the nervous system starts experiencing marked issues with personal organization, mood, and other distressing effects.[20]

5. **Has your son or daughter tried to reduce participation in game activities but found it *too difficult* to quit?** If the need for use has built up (high tolerance), decreases in the amount of use will be countered by the nervous system with withdrawal symptoms, which will erode the child's will to quit. For many children, abstinence or partial screen media use for only a week to ten days will begin to make it easier to decrease the amount of screen time required to avoid withdrawal symptoms. In terms of nervous system function, more time away from screen media makes it easier to quit. But getting through this acute stage of withdrawal takes resolve, and chronic screen dependence draws down the strength needed to quit.

6. **Has your son or daughter lost interest in non-game-related activities (e.g., sports, hobbies, family activities)?** If identity and neurologic development are proceeding normally, children show interest in a variety of activities that take them into their peer group and out into the

world, away from their parents. If **identity development** is hobbled by screen dependence, they shy away from anything that interferes with their screen time, including participation in sports, social activities, getting to know the opposite gender, working out, or learning to drive. In keeping with the progress of their screen dependence, activities and interests fall away one by one until the only thing left is screen time, and the only friends remaining are also involved in nonstop recreational screen media use.

7. **Has your son or daughter continued to engage in game activities despite knowing the problems they experience as a result of their use?** This question assesses for *salience of use.* Here we see, in a nutshell, the definition of destructive dependence contained in the phrase "continued use despite adverse consequences." Although the child knows that her or his screen dependence is unhealthy and retards cognitive function, nothing is done to moderate screen media use. Despite awareness of the destructive impacts of screen media overuse and the alarmed protestations of parents, as the child's dependence deepens, she or he loses interest in school, becomes depressed and unhealthy, and experiences marked difficulties in personal organization.

8. **Has your son or daughter deceived a family member, significant other, employer, or therapist regarding the amount of time spent engaging in gaming activities?** Lying about screen media use is done to protect access and quell questions adults may have about the amount of time a child spends with screen media. Screen-dependent children resist with all their might any attempts to curtail screen media use. They whine, fabricate the truth, pretend to be interested in things other than screen media, and

deploy countless manipulations to make sure that no one interferes with recreational screen media access. This behavior is part and parcel of addiction and dependence.

9. **Do you believe your son or daughter participates in gaming activities to feel better (e.g., reduce anxiety, loneliness, sadness, guilt, worry)?** One measure of the severity of any substance or practice dependence is the use of the substance or practice to self-medicate unpleasant feelings *caused by the dependency*. Rather than deal with anxiety, loneliness, or sadness, the child flees into screen media use and represses the painful feelings she or he experiences. Unfortunately, trying to run away from pain in this way only serves to deepen the child's misery. This is a phenomenon some writers term the "hamster wheel effect" of addiction and dependence—the more the person uses to self-medicate, the worse the dependence becomes, requiring still more self-medication or use.[21]

10. **Has your son or daughter jeopardized or lost an academic or employment opportunity or significant relationship because of their engagement with gaming activities?** Lean toward this being a problem if your child simply does not do homework, or if she or he does homework, does it so quickly, without reading directions properly, that the result is grossly unacceptable. Consider this factor also if your child does not do chores, or a teen does not leave the house to look for work. Staying home is the only way she or he can devote the greatest share of personal time and attention to screen media. Our client research has documented the presence of this factor in screen-dependent children and adults. In the case of adult users, we have witnessed them letting important

relationships in their personal and work lives wither so they can devote all their energy and attention to game play.

First document your child's screen dependence, then take action

Once you identify the presence of a screen dependency, you are in position to decide how rigorous screen controls should be. These could range from mild to severe. Examples of mild controls include agreements to turn off screen media at a prescribed time and to make homework and studying for school a priority. Examples of severe controls would be the use of a level system that allocates privileges based on strict compliance with standards of behavior, which are discussed in Chapter 11.

Screen-dependent children are as effective at hiding their dependence as people addicted to alcohol and other drugs. Typically screen-dependent children do not talk about screen overuse to people they suspect might identify dependence. The fact that children with compulsive screen media use issues lie to protect their access makes it unlikely that the children themselves will provide parents with an accurate measure of the degree of their dependence on screen media.

Given this situation, parents and other caregivers need to determine whether a child is successfully meeting established milestones for her or his cognitive, emotional, and social development. If lags are seen in any of these three domains, including a lack of emotional maturity, a drop in grades or disinterest in school, and a fractured social life, screen media overuse should be considered as a primary cause for the child's difficulties, and steps should be taken to decrease access to and use of screen media.

Once a child is identified as screen dependent, a marked decrease in use, or abstinence, should become the target state for parents. It is not an effective strategy to minimize the reality of the problem or suppose the child will eventually outgrow dependence. Our client research indicates that screen dependence simply deepens, as does the harm it does to the child's cognitive, emotional, and social capabilities. Unless caregivers push the situation by limiting use, there is no reason to believe that the problem will go away. Unpleasant as the task may be, it is better for caregivers to deal with the issue when it becomes evident. Not doing so only puts off the inevitable need for an encounter later in the child's life. Better to address the issue in elementary school or adolescence than deal with a child who cannot succeed at anything and falls behind peers in her or his twenties.

The good news is that children and young adults can heal from screen dependence if clear limits are applied in the context of strong parental resolve. This particular issue, as is the case with a poorly weeded garden, gets worse with neglect. Once the user gets the situation under control, recovery, not only remission of symptoms, is possible.

The need for package labeling

As was the case with cigarette smoking in the mid-twentieth century, damage done by screen dependence is greatly worsened by the public mythology that it is harmless. To the contrary, we believe that screen dependence is a public health hazard as great as that posed by dependence on opiates, alcohol, or nicotine.

The proliferation of screen media, as well as the tendency to design it to create compulsive use, has entranced the population gradually. Everyone is especially vulnerable to this public health challenge because it has crept up slowly, and when change happens slowly, people tend to not be very mindful of it. When video game companies first came out with *Mario Bros.* and other early entries, the medium seemed cute, fun, beguiling, and benign. It is no longer benign. But we see the damage it is doing every day in the families we serve. This is a problem that has crept up on these families, clouding parents' vision so they do not realize that something potentially destructive is happening in their lives, albeit quietly and slowly.

For this reason, we join with those parents calling for package labeling of purchasable screen media—in the box and through downloads. It is now well publicized that media companies hire staffs of psychologists to help them design games and other media with compulsion loops to increase the degree of psychological demand the game imposes on the player. This practice of deliberately making video games more addictive suggests that package labeling of this risk may be justified. Package labeling would give parents the information they need to decide whether a particular game might drive their already obsessive child to more extreme and impaired behavior.[22] There are currently no industry standards in this regard, but one measure would be statements such as "Using this game more than two hours a day has been shown to cause psychological and cognitive issues in children," or "Use of this medium is not advised for children with psychiatric diagnoses or learning disabilities."

A similar example of labeling is part of cigarette merchandising history in the United States. After much debate, the public realized that cigarettes were destructive, and the manufacturers knew about the dangers and were hiding them. Finally a law passed in 1966 mandating that proper labeling state the potential risks of smoking cigarettes.[23] Today, enough is known about screen dependence to realize that the screen media industry, too, should provide warnings because its consumers are mainly children.

Good news from the world of neurogenesis

Evidence from research on teen alcoholism suggests that if an adolescent can get control of substance dependence by the late teens, she or he may be able to grow into her or his twenties

31

without having to deal with a craving for alcohol.[24] If, on the other hand, a person continues to drink into her or his twenties and does decide to stop, it will be much more difficult. This bit of clinical wisdom gives us a solid basis for saying that controlling a child's screen dependence *now* may create long-term resistance to a *recurrence* of destructive recreational screen media use.

Turning to the field of neurogenesis—the study of how nerves are born and propagate in the brain—we learn that if we can get on top of an issue involving brain function early enough, the brain has an enormous plasticity and capability for self-healing.[25] But the problem needs to be addressed early. Chapter 2 discusses how chronic screen media use causes the release of destructive stress hormones that are corrosive and can damage structures in the brain connected with memory and learning.[26] Stress, depression, psychosis, and mania show the presence of a **kindling effect** that, if untreated, will result in a second experience of one of these states more harmful than the first one. A child who experiences chronic **meltdowns**—depression and anxiety expressed with manic force— over game play is actually damaging her or his brain.

But screen-dependent children are not left defenseless to brain deterioration by the kindling effect. Research also suggests that if intervention occurs early enough in the life cycle of depression—if a stressor is addressed early enough or a substance dependency is stopped early enough, as in the case of teen alcoholism—there is a very good chance the individual will be able to banish the specific dependency forever. Therefore, the boundaries and structures—the tough love—you give your child now can have big payoffs later.

CHAPTER 2

Brains Awash in Adrenaline: What Overclocking the Brain Does to the Bodies, Minds, and Nervous Systems of Screen-Dependent Children

"We design our games to hook them in. Part of the hook is how we build the games—to deliberately overclock their minds. Most people think at about 600 words a minute. We make them think at 1,000 words a minute."

This revelation was said in the course of a conversation with an executive of a large gaming company. This man thought that there was nothing wrong with what he was doing. In fact, he said, "We hire PhDs in psychology to help engineer our games to be successful—to get kids stuck on them."

In order for a video game or other screen medium to be financially successful, two things in terms of brain function should occur: it must be fun, which increases the availability of pleasure neurons in the brain, and it must create a strong tendency toward *compulsive* use. A screen medium must contain what game manufacturers term *compulsion loops,* meaning the game is programmed to pull children into the play and then repeatedly frustrate them while offering incremental rewards as play proceeds through various levels.[27]

To build brain dependence on a particular screen medium, use of the medium has to be exciting. In terms of function of the human nervous system, it has to trigger the **general adaptation syndrome (GAS),** the "fight-or-flight" stress reaction pattern. When the GAS comes on, it blows vast amounts of **adrenaline** into the nervous system.

Child and adolescent clients with bipolar disorder, as well as those with an issue with screen dependence, say they can actually feel adrenaline as heat rising upward from the midriff. Adrenaline is felt as excitement.[28] It is this excitement that pulls the child into a pattern of chronic screen use and dependence.

The brain develops long-term dependence on screen media use through the accumulation of the chemical precursor to adrenaline, which is **dopamine.** The following diagram provides an overview of how dopamine leads to dependence over time.

CHRONIC SCREEN MEDIA USE AND THE BRAIN

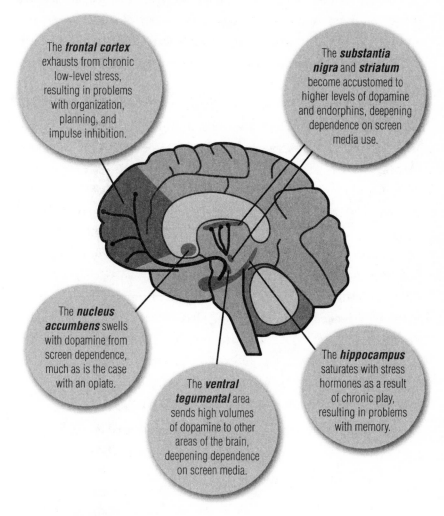

The **frontal cortex** exhausts from chronic low-level stress, resulting in problems with organization, planning, and impulse inhibition.

The **substantia nigra** and **striatum** become accustomed to higher levels of dopamine and endorphins, deepening dependence on screen media use.

The **nucleus accumbens** swells with dopamine from screen dependence, much as is the case with an opiate.

The **ventral tegumental** area sends high volumes of dopamine to other areas of the brain, deepening dependence on screen media.

The **hippocampus** saturates with stress hormones as a result of chronic play, resulting in problems with memory.

The Serotonin Connection

Chronic play also impacts another of the brain's important neurotransmitters: *serotonin*, called "the civilizing neurotransmitter." Too much recreational screen media use at night causes changes in how the brain uses serotonin and regulates the sleep-wake cycle. This leads to sleep problems, depression, anxiety, and vulnerability to suicidal thinking.

Dependence on a particular medium follows the chronic release of adrenaline. Even if the child becomes angry or frustrated playing a particular video game, the experience of adrenaline while in this angry state is felt as pleasurable. Many of the children and adolescents we work with tell us that it feels *good* to get *really angry*. For them, breaking things in a fit of angry frustration while playing a video game has a payoff.

The payoff is an elevation in adrenaline, which feels good. The more adrenaline released, the greater the dependence. Research suggests that a **massive multiplayer online role-playing game (MMORPG)** is the most adrenalizing screen medium; examples are *League of Legends, World of Warcraft,* and *Clash of Clans.*[29] But children may also become dependent on the experience of their minds floating through hours of YouTube videos or surfing on Twitter or Snapchat as a behavior-shaping force, pushing their behavior in certain predictable directions.

As adrenaline goes up, the brain goes into hyperdrive, and the child experiences a period of enhanced focus on his screen media. As screen media use continues uninterrupted for hours, more disturbing results are seen. Research shows that these media present highly arousing, abnormal sensory input to the brain's activating system.[30] Downstream effects of this arousal include

- a *markedly* decreased attention span;
- an increase in brain-metabolism patterns similar to that seen in drug addicts;
- an increase in short-term aggression (for violent video games), especially in younger children and boys, along with an increased likelihood of later antisocial behavior;
- deterioration of **brain executive function** (remembering, planning, and inhibiting impulsivity);
- increased vigilance, irritability, and depression;[31]
- sleep disorders;[32]

- development of anxiety disorders;[33]
- the risk of receiving a diagnosis of ADHD at age seven that increases with every hour of media use for young children.

How chronic screen media use pushes disorganization and mood drop

If a child uses recreational screen media for more than an hour a day, some of the downstream effects noted in the previous section will start to materialize.[34] The brain can deal with screen media use in moderation, but if it is pushed by a compulsion loop, damage will occur. Chronic excessive screen time eventually exhausts the brain with the buildup of **corticotropin-releasing factor (CRF)** that accompanies adrenaline. This neurochemical kicks the brain into high gear when so commanded by the stress reaction and stimulates the release of cortisol. Cortisol pushes the nervous system into action, but if stress goes on chronically, the presence of cortisol can result in damage to the brain's memory circuits and other structures tasked to attention, mood, and impulse control.[35]

As stated earlier, brain executive function is impacted by chronic screen overuse. Stress retards the function of the brain center tasked for memory, the **hippocampus,** and when this happens the child's **short-term memory** will start slipping. He will forget things and become disorganized. His ability to think efficiently and solve problems or remember basic facts will slip. Homework hour becomes "hell hour," with his parents trapped in the role of suspicious overseers.[36]

The brain can heal, but it needs time and cessation of the hyperadrenalized state for a period to recharge. If it does not get this relief, the kindling effect begins, causing the deterioration of brain structures associated with mood stability. Chronic play causes the child to experience anxiety and a mild-to-moderate irritable depression. Research on the impact of these mood states suggests that if depression or anxiety remains untreated, it becomes worse over time; the "slow burn" of chronic stress eventually engulfs the brain.[37]

Unlike its manifestation in adults, depression in children is more likely to be expressed in rage or chronic irritability than in sadness, lethargy, or a sense of futility.[38] Many children demonstrate a tendency toward violent anger when frustrated during game play or if prevented by parents from accessing media. (This rage is not indicative of any tendency to physically attack others.) This enraged behavior may look similar to the actions of people diagnosed with bipolar disorder who are experiencing a mixed state of extreme anger, extreme impulsivity, and extreme dark mood expressed with manic force.[39]

Lifestyle impacts of screen dependence

In order to assess lifestyle impacts of chronic recreational screen media use, we analyzed a randomly chosen group of 117 children for whom we had detailed client and family records. This analysis suggested the presence of a distinct pattern of lifestyle impacts caused by screen dependence:

- failure in school or greatly suboptimum performance

- moderate to severe apathy; no life goals for the child

- loss of face-to-face friendship networks and a marked decrease in social confidence

- disruption of **attachment** patterns with parents

- development of narcissistic and grandiose personality features—a child may be failing three out of five subjects in school and still maintain that he is above all this busy work, and a sense of cool arrogance appears, even in younger children

- disruption of normal identity formation processes, resulting in painful inability to make important decisions—the child has no sense of self

- difficulty envisioning any future—the child has no personal imagination of her or his own potential greatness

- use of manipulative strategies employed by addicts, including lying, stealing, and threats of violence

A solid causal link between screen media use and *assaultive behavior*—violence directed toward others in the child's community—has not been established in the research. But it is clear that certain children have a special vulnerability to developing a more violent perspective as a result of violent screen media use. These include children from abusive environments, those on the autistic spectrum, and any child who, for any reason, is friendless and lonely and/or ignored by his parents.

In terms of real damage, the problem is not that screen media overuse makes children violent, but rather that it makes them depressed, anxious, and intellectually incapable of realizing their potential. Screen media overuse attacks the brain and damages it directly more than it causes children to behave violently.

The impact on muscle development and boys' "weakness syndrome"

One of the remarkable and dramatic aspects of screen dependence that we have noticed in our clients is the screen-dependent child's general look of physical weakness. This is specific to boys; it looks as if there is no timbre, no strength, no resilience or stability in their bodies. John McKinnon, who is a sought-after fitness trainer in the Seattle area with over thirty years' experience, told us that he is quite familiar with this look of weakness in boys, which has to do with them not using their bodies for anything that requires exertion.[40]

Sadly, McKinnon reports, the bodies of the gamer kids he works with are not maturing normally. He notes that if a child spends all his time in a darkened room, he does not experience muscle challenge; therefore, he does not express normal levels of testosterone in his body. No expression of testosterone means stunted muscle development. The boy or young man loses his muscle tone as would someone confined in a hospital bed for a long period. Boys and men whose bodies express this **weakness syndrome**

- have a distinct posture that includes shoulders rolled forward, back hunched, and chest caved in (McKinnon calls this the "gamer body"), and their breath is shallow, which can be a cause of why they are so anxious—they are not breathing deeply but are in a chronic state of hyperadrenalized shallow breathing;

- flap their arms and hands in trying to soothe the carpel tunnel syndrome they are experiencing, or show presence of *gamer's thumb*—chronic inflammation and soreness from overuse of the game controller;

- have poor coordination, which McKinnon emphasizes is signatory of this condition;

- look androgynous, thin, even emaciated until their mid-twenties, at which time they begin putting on weight and continue to show poor self-care habits;

- are afraid of girls and maturing sexually (given that a large percentage of screen-dependent boys also use porn, the issue of sexual maturity is complicated by how porn portrays women);[41]

- age quicker due to fatigue of the adrenal system as a result of chronic stress—some boys will actually look older than their age;

- experience more injuries because they lack muscle development—muscles absorb shock, and without muscles deeper damage can occur.

McKinnon observes an interesting cross-cultural phenomenon: Asians are getting taller than westerners because their diets are getting better generationally. It used to be the other way around.[42] Now, the availability of junk food in the United States has degraded the health of our youth so much that children are actually growing up *shorter.*

After observing this effect, McKinnon notes that he has more tolerance for expressions of anger by leaders of other countries in Asia about the "toxic" impact of American culture. A lot of people are making money selling video games and fast food in China, but not everyone there is happy about it. This may also contribute to why the Chinese and South Korean governments run military-style rehabilitation camps for children who have been identified as compulsive video game users. These countries see screen dependence as a national health issue so the government, not parents, makes the decision as to whether a child is picked up and sent away for rehabilitation.[43] On the bright side, McKinnon reports, girls' athletics is jumping ahead of boys' sports worldwide. Males are losing the competitive edge that testosterone has traditionally given them.

According to McKinnon, the "everyone gets a trophy" philosophy that has figured in children's athletics in the last quarter century or so is also part of the problem. Real athletic achievement is not rewarded if the primary criterion used is "Will not getting this trophy hurt my child's self-esteem?" Suffice it to say that if parents are afraid of letting their children experience pain, these children will never know how to deal with it themselves.

From the parents' perspective

Most screen-dependent children do not meet the mental illness criteria of being a "danger to self and others" or "gravely impaired." A particular child's enjoyment of his screen media may delight parents, and they may feel a lot of conflict in limiting his play. They are forced to ask themselves if there is something else he should be doing. If he is not hurting himself, taking drugs, or breaking the law, why should they get involved in what he does in his spare time?

As parents ponder this dilemma, they may become aware of a still, small voice that tells them that their child is never really *present* with them anymore. They may find themselves wondering where their bright, happy, mischievous, sometimes devious, but rarely deliberately manipulative boy went. They note that now he is not fun to be around. And they constantly have to deal with his attempts to cleverly get them to give him more screen access and get off his back about anything else, including his schoolwork.

Many parents also notice that something has happened to their child's sense of imagination that feels unsettling. No longer does he sit out on the porch at night or lie on the grass looking up at the stars, wondering. That light has gone out. No longer does he enjoy biking around the neighborhood with his buddies. Now he stares absently at them and tells them his creativity and imagination have improved because he is learning the storyline of his game and how to think like the person who wrote the game so he can win. In truth, his play has not developed his imagination. He is simply using someone else's imagination, going through the levels, living in a plastic (and often violent) virtual world.

From the healthcare provider's perspective

We hear many gamer kids voicing a peculiar sense of superiority, as seen in the mythical "superiority complex" we used to hear about. The child believes that because he is a good game player, he is extraordinarily competent in other domains of endeavor. This characteristic is especially seen in the screen-dependent child who is not making the grade at school and may look at school as busy work. He typically foregoes studying, believing that he can pull off an A on tests—even though he cannot—and is very apathetic about everything other than gaming.

In terms of behavior, we observe social awkwardness in screen-dependent children as might be seen in a child on the autism spectrum. They lack social confidence or think other children are talking about them. They are unassertive socially and do not know how to do anything unless it has to do with their screen pursuits. They look and act disturbingly younger than their chronological age.

And there is a lot of yawning and mumbling. Cynthia tells the children she tutors that she has a built-in **yawn-o-meter.** She ventures that she can give them a good estimate on how many hours of sleep they got the night before by the number of yawns she counts per session. She is very good at using humor to establish rapport with children, and, in turn, they tell her the truth. Usually it is something like "Yeah, I was up until 3 a.m. texting with my friends. I kept myself awake with Diet Coke," or "I was on a raid with my *World of Warcraft* clan."

We are what we eat. If we feed our brains positive challenge and real-world experience, we tend to get bigger in spirit, happier, and better at what we do. If we feed our brains violence and mush, years of consuming the "empty calories" of screen dependence, we get self-contempt, crippling apathy, and physical weakness.

The impacts of screen dependence through the child's twenties

Currently, there isn't much research on the outcomes, i.e., what happens to hard-core screen media users as they grow through their twenties and thirties. Right now, a review of our client experience (approximately 500 children) suggests that many children and young adults challenged with screen dependence do not get out of the house until their late twenties. If they go to college, they may not make it past their sophomore year because of the pressure of their screen dependence and the damage that it has done to them in terms of knowledge not gained in high school. Many go to college, waste a couple of years and perhaps $60,000 of their parents' money, and drop out. Spending too much time in an artificial world has the disadvantage of not teaching a child how to survive out in the world where people actually put expectations on her or him for difficult task accomplishment.

So the eventual outcome for some screen-dependent young adults will be a loss of energy, capability, and opportunity. Many do extricate themselves from the absolute grip of screen dependence in their late twenties, but by this age, so much time has been wasted. It is rough to graduate from college or begin work with people six to eight years younger than you are.

What is your bottom line?

A client was in a fifteen-year psychologically abusive marriage. She had not taken a stand against her husband's behavior because she still believed she could "change him with love." During one of his visits, the client's brother witnessed her husband berating her. Her brother said two things that changed her life: "I didn't know you were afraid of him," and "What is your bottom line?" Several days later, the client filed for divorce. It took certain key words to bounce her out of her lifelong "love conquers all" trance, but once those words were uttered, her wiser self emerged.

To restate the theme from the Introduction and quote the renowned psychotherapist Dr. Erving Polster, "What we do grows on us."[44] No one is to blame here. Everyone is truly doing the best that they can given the information they have. Unfortunately, most of the information we, the parents, get about media is from the companies selling the media. Now parents are getting new information from doing their own research and connecting the dots. Contrary to the view promulgated by the media industry, this new research tells us that *screen dependence can damage a person's nervous system.* The numbers are in.

So we ask you, "What is your bottom line?" As you ponder your own correct action in this situation and look for evidence of damage from screen dependence, please consider more than the hard-core traditional mental illness metrics of "danger to self" or "gravely impaired." Reflect upon how you want your child's mind, body, and spirit to develop. Consider whether you want him to build his personal autobiography, his identity, from real experience or from his virtual experience playing video games and using other digital media. Do you want him to grow up in the real world or the artificial world promulgated by the media industry?

Your child's nervous system is enormously capable of self-repair. The human brain is a marvelous work-in-progress, and everything we do or learn results in physical changes in brain structure. This means that the new standards of behavior you establish today begin having payoffs for your child's well-being *today*!

CHAPTER 3

There Is No Pill to Cure It: How to Know Whether the Problem Is Caused by Screen Dependence or a Co-occurring Psychiatric Condition

Many parents of a child with a screen dependence issue also suspect that the child has a learning disability (a brain-based inability to read, write, or do mathematics) or psychiatric illness, such as attention-deficit/hyperactivity disorder (ADHD), depression, bipolar disorder, **generalized anxiety disorder (GAD), or autism spectrum disorder (ASD).** Before you can help your child, you have to know how his lack of success is or is not caused by the screen dependence and what part of it is secondary to the presence of a childhood psychiatric condition or a learning disability.

If your child is truly ADHD, medication and modification of his educational plan at school will be genuinely helpful, and you will see clear results. If he is truly depressed, antidepressant-medication management along with cognitive-behavioral psychotherapy may be parts of the solution. If he suffers from pediatric bipolar disorder, mood-stabilizing medication along with specific supports at home and school are essential. If he *does not* suffer from these conditions, that fact should be documented so it is clear that resolution of the issue should not involve medication but rather your child's self-directed behavior change.

Most of the children who come to counseling with an identified screen dependence issue carry one or more of the previously listed diagnoses, so it is not at all unusual for a screen-dependent child to have some co-occurring condition as well. The best research indicates that the potential to express these conditions is largely inherited.[45] But it should be noted that other environmental and postnatal events can cause all the symptoms listed in the *DSM-5* for the conditions that will be discussed in this chapter. These events include traumatic brain injury, hypoxia at birth, parents' use of alcohol or other drugs, childhood diseases, and traumatic stress.[46]

The potential for a child to become screen dependent may also be related to genetics, such as when a parent has a substance abuse issue or a substance dependency.[47] But the child's screen dependence is neither inherited nor caused by environmental factors—it is the result of choices that the child made and continues to make every day. It is potentially reversible. Psychiatric conditions may greatly improve over time, but they do not go away. Neither do learning disabilities, such as dyslexia. But with proper management, there is no reason why a child cannot completely recover from screen dependence.

Can a child acquire one of the conditions as a result of chronic screen use?

There is good evidence from research that chronic screen media use can cause a child to develop symptoms that would qualify him for the diagnosis of ADHD, depression, or anxiety and could qualify him for a diagnosis on the autistic spectrum or of **intermittent explosive disorder (IED).** With regard to ADHD, research states that the chance a child will later be diagnosed with the disorder goes up in direct proportion to the amount of daily recreational screen media use he has experienced since the age of three.[48]

Doctors rarely diagnose bipolar disorder in children for fear of the stigma associated with the diagnosis. The intermittent explosive disorder diagnosis appeared in the *DSM-5* in 2013 and settled the argument temporarily about whether there is such a thing as manic-depression in children. A child with IED will demonstrate unpremeditated rage—a near-psychotic attack on his surroundings that can be a core symptom of mania in bipolar disorder. Dr. Demitri Popolos, an authority on bipolar disorder in children, provides an accurate characterization of the mood of children with bipolar disorder, stating that they have a low threshold for frustration in situations that require sustained attention, interest, and effort; a tendency to become overaroused, anxious, or fearful when exposed to novel sensory stimulation and/or setting of limits; impatience; impulsivity; and inability to delay immediate gratification.[49]

There is no current longitudinal research that provides evidence that behaviors and mood states associated with screen dependence *remain* after cessation of destructive screen media use. But when we look at how the brain grows and repairs itself, we see that early intervention is important. If early intervention does not occur, the symptoms associated with all the disorders listed in the following sections will continue. And the human brain will eventually acclimate to a steady state—in which adrenaline and other neurochemicals achieve and maintain stability in their strengths and interactions. As the pioneering neuropsychologist Dr. Donald Hebb puts it, "Neurons that fire together wire together."[50]

Importantly, there is no medication, no fail-safe therapeutic protocol or educational accommodation that can remit symptoms of a screen dependency. There are dozens of medications that provide genuine help to children with psychiatric illness, therapeutic protocols, and IEP accommodations that can help children with inherited learning disabilities or psychiatric issues, but nothing exists for screen dependence.

The fundamental importance of a good educational assessment

Your child's teacher will tell you that the first step in helping him at school is getting a good **educational assessment,** which is a test battery that gives a measure of his social and emotional issues, his intelligence quotient (the relationship of his intellectual age to his chronological age), his learning disabilities, if any, and recommendations for remediation. This will be the first thing your child's school will do in the special education planning process. If the assessment reveals learning disabilities or emotional problems that interfere with academic progress, a formal IEP is created.

Getting a good educational assessment is the first order of business in determining whether screen dependence is involved in a child's struggles because it reveals whether a genuine learning disability is the issue or he is sabotaging himself with screen dependence. The assessment can also point toward the presence of disabling psychiatric conditions, such as ADHD, a mood disorder, or autism. For ADHD, look for problems in *processing speed, inattention, and short-term auditory-memory issues.* If a mood disorder is suspect, review parts of the test battery that address *emotional difficulties.* If autism is suspected, pay careful attention to test results that indicate difficulty in *interpersonal communications and understanding of day-to-day social pragmatics*—how to get along with others, make friends, and keep friends.[51]

If the educational assessment suggests that your child has one or more learning disabilities or disabling conditions, an IEP will be written to address these issues. If it does not suggest the presence of learning disabilities, look hard at the possibility that a screen dependency is the core difficulty and begin planning implementation of screen controls at home and school.

A closer look at comparison conditions

In terms of helping your child with impairments in function at home and school, clarity changes everything. Once you know what is going on, you are able to position your approach so you do not make things worse. You want every strategy you use to have the maximum force in terms of helping your child. If one of the following conditions *is* present, you will need to make treatment a priority and take it into account in everything you do as a parent.

Conversely, the illusion that a genuine psychiatric condition, not screen dependence, is the cause of problems can slow down your enforcement of screen controls. After all, if your child has a psychiatric disability, he is only partially in control. The wrong explanation gives him a good excuse and prevents change from happening as quickly as it should and could happen.

This being said, client experience informs us that many parents, even when it is clear that a child has a genuine psychiatric condition, do not pursue medication because they fear side effects. Or they may resist having the child diagnosed because they do not want their child labeled with a diagnosis from the *DSM-5*. This reluctance is understandable but can have the consequence of preventing a child from getting the help he needs, when he needs it. Early intervention is key. Late intervention can make the situation worse.

ADHD

Attention-deficit/hyperactivity disorder (ADHD) is a complex attentional disorder marked by issues with short-term memory and attention, distractibility, impulsivity, hyperactivity, and brain activation—the brains of children with ADHD do not light up for uninteresting tasks. They are motivated by what is interesting, not what is important.[52]

- **Prevalence:** 9 to 10 percent of children. Unless otherwise stated, the prevalence levels noted for the diagnoses listed in this chapter are derived from studies of these conditions in children in the United States.[53]

- **Major challenges:** ADHD children tend to be slower mental processors—it takes them longer to solve problems. They have difficulty mastering any learning task that is not intrinsically interesting. They typically have difficulty organizing themselves and meeting time-specific commitments. And a cycling mild depression called *dysthymia* may be present, marked by frequent, sometimes sudden, drops from a normal mood to a somewhat depressed mood.[54]

- **Typical school accommodations:** Most ADHD children will benefit from accommodations in Section 504 of the Rehabilitation Act. They will be given more time to complete academic work and testing. They may receive priority seating in the classroom to minimize distractibility. Children with ADHD should also be tested to determine whether they have reading and math issues. These problems are caused by their typically lower-than-average short-term memory spans. This learning disability will qualify them for extra one-to-one or pullout instruction delivered through an IEP.

- **Typical home accommodations:** ADHD children need directions broken down into individual steps in a sequence. Tasks and homework assignments need to be chunked into manageable sizes so that the child can do as much of the task as he can at one sitting without becoming frustrated and oppositional. ADHD children need help with personal organization, with the first order of business being a thorough education in the use of a large, written

planner for organizing each week. (For more on planners, refer to Chapter 6.) Digital handheld devices are not visual enough for them and do not require personal notation, which, in itself, is a memory prompt. They need to develop routines and structures and get in the habit of doing things right now so as to sidestep their ADHD-related tendency for procrastination.

How ADHD and screen dependence are different		
ISSUE OR SYMPTOM	AS AN ASPECT OF ADHD	AS AN ASPECT OF SCREEN DEPENDENCE
Difficulty in mastering any learning task that is not intrinsically interesting.	Relates to a neurologically based brain activation issue: the brain does not pay attention to stimuli that have not been tagged as part of an interesting pattern.	Chronic screen media use has trained the brains of children to crave excitement. Renders children incapable of focusing on anything but screen pursuits.
Very poor personal organization.	Relates primarily to deficits in short-term memory, distractibility, and attention.	Relates to deliberately putting a high action priority only on recreational screen media use.
Poor brain executive function.	Is a result of lifelong challenges related to brain development and function, with a strongly inherited component.	Is a result of the child's constant rumination about his screen media and sleep deprivation related to its use. He could focus if he wanted to.
Presence of dysthymia.	May result from difficulty getting a sense of reward from small, daily successes and enjoyments because the brain's dopaminergic system is impaired.	Results from a buildup of frustration as the child attempts to complete compulsion loops designed into his recreational screen media.

How ADHD and screen dependence are different (continued)		
ISSUE OR SYMPTOM	AS AN ASPECT OF ADHD	AS AN ASPECT OF SCREEN DEPENDENCE
Slowed mental processing; it takes longer to read, do math problems, and accomplish other mental tasks (even in the presence of a superior IQ).	A direct result of being born with ADHD and measured as problematic in most IQ tests completed by ADHD children.	A result of rumination on screen media pursuits and sleep deprivation.
Neurological testing reveals that stimulant medication helps the ADHD brain focus better.	Stimulant medication helps ADHD children overcome executive function deficits.	Medication has little impact on screen-dependent children with no ADHD on board. A result of brain exhaustion and sleep deprivation.

To distinguish screen dependence from ADHD as a cause for issues, consider the following questions:

- Did the child show the presence of these challenges *before* he began actively overusing screen media? If so, think ADHD.

- Do these issues clear up when his screen access is limited and his sleep schedule is restored? If so, think screen dependence.

- Does stimulant medication make a difference? If so, think ADHD.

- Can he pay attention if he is rested and free of the stress caused by screen media overuse? If yes, think screen dependence.

- Can he do uninteresting things when he puts his mind to it? One way to informally assess for screen dependence is to ask a child what excites him. If he immediately mentions his recreational screen media, there is a good chance he has issues with its use. Think screen dependence.

- Do IQ subtests that measure short-term memory and processing speed suggest the presence of an attention deficit? Problems with short-term memory suggest ADHD.[55]

DEPRESSION

Depression is one of the most common mental disorders in the United States. A major depressive episode is defined as a period of two weeks or longer during which there is either a depressed mood or loss of interest or pleasure and at least four other symptoms that reflect a change in functioning, such as problems with sleep, eating, energy, concentration, and self-image.[56] Depression emerges differently in adolescents than it does in adults. Typically, adolescents demonstrate a chronic irritability coupled with problems getting a good night's sleep. The depressed adolescent becomes isolated from friends, athletics, and other interests.[57]

- **Prevalence:** 11 percent of children, with a third of this group being female.

- **Major challenges:** Depressed children and teens typically have poor stress resistance and tend to be inflexible, black-and-white thinkers. When depression hits, they may become intellectually disabled: they forget what they are doing at school, go blank during tests, or are crippled by high anxiety and gloom-and-doom thoughts. Depression is a *mind and body pain syndrome:* experience is painful, movement is painful, and mood is dark and tearful.

- **Typical school accommodations:** School-related issues of depressed children may be helped by antidepressant medication. And, depending on the severity of the depressive disorder, a child may require home or hospital tutoring services. Although not directly addressed in federal law—states vary in how they comply with the requirement for home-based services—home/hospital educational services are typically provided if a student cannot attend school because of a disabling condition, and the school district *must* provide certified staff for home-based tutoring.[58] At school, depressed children and adolescents need a great deal of attention and support to get through the day, with flexibility at the start of the school day as well as IEP provisions for reduced academic requirements.

- **Typical home accommodations:** Depressed children need to be able to talk with parents and get reassurance that things will improve. Parents serve best by helping the child envision ways to be resourceful in dealing with depressive affect. They will point to things the child has done or can do in the future to get her or his life back on track. It is not a good idea to demonize a depressive state, relating to it as a crippling disease. A child's depression should not be a pass to miss school, skip household chores and homework, or avoid ongoing training in self-responsibility. The question for a parent always must be: "What can I do to keep things moving forward?" Adequate sleep is an essential part of healing from depression, as are opportunities for athletic participation and daily exercise.

How depression and screen dependence are different

ISSUE OR SYMPTOM	AS AN ASPECT OF DEPRESSION	AS AN ASPECT OF SCREEN DEPENDENCE
Chronic irritability.	A direct result of the disorder and sleep deprivation.	A result of sleep deprivation and chronic frustration when using screen media.
Poor hygiene.	When depressed, does not bathe, brush hair or teeth, etc.	Accesses media for many hours in one sitting and does not stop to bathe.
Poor diet and physical impairments related to malnutrition.	When depressed, experiences greatly diminished appetite.	Eats primarily sweets, refined carbohydrates, and energy drinks.
Chronic sleep issues.	A direct result of the disorder; often accompanied by high nighttime worry.	Nighttime media access eventually causes disruption of the circadian rhythms and the sleep-awake daily cycle.
Fatigue, sadness, and hyperemotionality.	Depression is an emotional pain syndrome; these are lifelong challenges.	A direct result of the chronic low-level stress experienced with screen media use.
Cognitive impairment and hyposomniac retardation (moving and thinking slowly, as if in a trance).	Caused by exhaustion of the nervous system as a result of depression.	Caused by sleep deprivation, brain exhaustion, and loss of opportunity for real-world academic and social learning.
Antidepressant medication may help.	Helps some percentage of children with depression.	Has no direct effect on depression-like behavior.

Are most screen-dependent children genuinely depressed as a result of their compulsive screen media use? Our clinical observations suggest that these children tend to be less depressed and more chronically *frustrated* by the inability to experience a stable sense of satisfaction from their screen media involvement or game play. Remember, video games now contain built-in compulsion loops. The frustration a child experiences with these dynamics may give him the bitter demeanor of a grouchy, depressed older person. If a child's primary screen dependence involves social media (more girls than boys fall into this category), depression may be a direct result of social rejection and online bullying.[59]

To distinguish screen dependence from depression as a cause for issues, consider the following questions:

- Did the depressive state emerge before he started using recreational screen media? If so, think depression.

- If the child is not getting enough sleep, why is he staying awake too late? Is he using media or trying to get to sleep but cannot? If it is media, think screen dependence. If not, consider that depression is the issue.

- Has the child experienced some trauma, such as the loss of function from an accident or a head injury? Trauma may cause depression in the hours or days following the experience. If so, consider that factors other than screen dependence may be involved.

- Does the child seem angry when he is depressed? Many children who overuse screen media eventually develop a caustic, depressive attitude that looks like clinical depression but may be the chronic irritability that comes from too much screen media use.

- Does the child's depression fade when he is talking about his favorite screen media? When she or he is home ill, do symptoms fade? If so, think screen dependence.

ANXIETY

Anxiety is the experience of vague dread that something bad is going to happen without having a clear idea of what that would be. It is an aversive emotion that mobilizes the mind and the body to avoid stressful situations. Body referents are stomach upset, vague feelings of discomfort, headache, and loss of focus. Mental referents include a vague pessimism about any novel activity. Children experience social anxiety, separation anxiety (typically a child cannot stand to be out of contact with a parent), body image anxiety, social humiliation anxiety, anxiety about being hurt, anxious coping, and perfectionism.[60]

- **Prevalence:** 15 to 20 percent of children.

- **Major challenges:** Children challenged by anxiety may resist going to school and develop stomachaches, headaches, or extreme resistance to getting out the door in the morning. At school, socially anxious children are not able to speak in front of others, answer questions, make presentations, or participate in social activities. They lack the courage to do these things and may experience powerful loneliness and a sense of isolation. If an anxiety state results in staying home too much, they may quickly become agoraphobic, which is the experience of dread involved in leaving their room or home or going out to be among people in stores, restaurants, or recreational settings.

- **Typical school accommodations:** Anxious children at school need a lot of predictability, structure, and help with self-organization. They do not do well with surprise activities and do not work well when teamed up with other children. They need extra time on tests and encouragement to complete tests and assignments. They withdraw and freeze up mentally if confronted directly by teachers or embarrassed in front of other children. If possible, the child should be invited to be involved in athletics at school. Movement, which gets children out of their heads and into their bodies, is an essential curative for anxiety.

- **Typical home accommodations:** Children do well when parents allow an anxious child to complete tasks on his or her own schedule and do not scold or push too hard with chores. The anxious child will benefit from predictability, routine, and structure in daily life. These children need to be given choices rather than directives for task accomplishment as well as more time to accomplish tasks. Children tormented by anxiety should get adequate sleep and exercise.

How anxiety and screen dependence are different

ISSUE OR SYMPTOM	AS AN ASPECT OF ANXIETY	AS AN ASPECT OF SCREEN DEPENDENCE
Acts aversively when confronted with any novel situation.	Could reflect a combination of subtypes of anxiety, including social anxiety or harm avoidance.	Chronic rapid triggering of the stress syndrome through game play results in oversensitization to new stimuli.
School refusal.	Expresses high social anxiety, humiliation and rejection anxiety, or harm avoidance.	Oversensitization of brain caused by chronic low-level stress may lead to marked social anxiety.
Excessive worry.	Caused by overactivity of brain centers tasked for vigilance.	Too much experience with game compulsion loops.
Agoraphobia.	Expresses harm avoidance.	Nonstop impulse to use screen media.
Meltdowns when frustrated, depressed, or anxious.	Typically these express reactive aggression: the child feels threatened and lashes out.	Temper dyscontrol caused by chronic frustration with game compulsion loops. Not reactive aggression.
Oppositionality.	The brain's attention centers, overwhelmed by anxiety, put on the brakes.	Fear of losing control of screen media access.
Trouble getting to sleep or getting enough sleep.	"Worry loops" torment the minds of most anxious children at night. Their minds incessantly flit from one worrisome thought to another.	Child stays up or gets up in the middle of the night to access recreational screen media.

To distinguish screen dependence from anxiety as a cause for issues, consider the following questions:

- Did the child have the issues/symptoms described in the first column of the table before getting into chronic recreational screen media use? If so, there is a higher likelihood that an onboard anxiety disorder is present.

- Are meltdowns or anxious withdrawal from others related to denial of screen media access? If so, consider that screen dependence is the culprit.

- Does the child strive to be successful in school and get good grades in tutoring or other instructional settings? If he is motivated to succeed, there is a greater chance that problems are related to an onboard anxiety syndrome or disorder and not directly related to screen dependence.

- Does the child appear to be trying to sleep at night or is he using screen media (even if he says it makes him sleepy)? If he is trying to sleep but cannot, anxiety may be the issue.

EARLY-ONSET BIPOLAR DISORDER/INTERMITTENT EXPLOSIVE DISORDER (IED)

Bipolar disorder is characterized by difficulty regulating good and bad moods as well as controlling impulsivity and maintaining mental focus. In adults, clear states of mania and depression are observed. Mania is an inappropriately elevated mood—feeling too good, too optimistic, and too capable. Bipolar disorder manifests differently in children; there are rage fits (described in the *DSM-5* as intermittent explosive disorder), extreme and sometimes dangerous hyperactivity, chronic irritability, extreme impulsivity, and, in many cases, hypersexuality.[61] Bipolar disorder is a serious mental illness and often is accompanied by psychotic phenomena such as hallucinations (visual hallucinations are more common than auditory hallucinations), delusions (irrational beliefs about things), and paranoia (the sense that one is in danger and must constantly be on the lookout for threats). In adolescents, the first stage of bipolar disorder may be chronic, extreme irritability.[62]

- **Prevalence:** 1 to 2 percent of children.

- **Major challenges:** Children challenged by bipolar disorder typically have no sense of personal identity. Developing a sense of self requires insight and predictability, two qualities missing in the lives of children with this disorder. They report feeling lost in a mental fog, driven by mental and physical hyperactivity that far exceeds that seen in ADHD (although some 80 percent of children with a primary diagnosis of bipolar disorder also qualify for an ADHD diagnosis). While they may typically be tested with IQs in the superior range, they have an extremely difficult time using their brainpower because they cannot hold focus. They experience mental hyperactivity, termed "flight of ideas," which describes the inability to sort, order, and focus sequentially on one idea at a time.[63]

- **Typical school accommodations:** Children with bipolar disorder need to be on mood-stabilizing and antipsychotic medication; this medication has a variety of impacts at school including cognitive dulling, the need for frequent urination, sensitivity to heat and light, tremors, and difficulty with any kind of physical exertion. These side effects need to be described in the child's IEP, and specific accommodations need to be written into that plan to help him through his school day. Many children with bipolar disorder also experience cognitive issues similar to ADHD and need similar types of Section 504 and IEP accommodations that are afforded children who have difficulties with short-term memory, distractibility, and inattention. Finally, the child's problems with impulsivity and low-level social paranoia may cause him to do things that get him in trouble and result in his social isolation. Because of these issues, success at school will most likely involve frequent communication among teachers, parents, and therapists involved in the child's life.

- **Typical home accommodations:** Research suggests that the best home environments for children with bipolar disorder are structured, predictable, and very positive. In these homes, parents work together to ensure that the child knows what is expected of him. They are firm and follow up on stated consequences. Children suffering from bipolar disorder need firm structure. These children also need daily role modeling on how to solve problems without drama, how to be positive and resourceful when one is depressed and miserable, and how to keep moving forward in life. Parents should use positive verbal and nonverbal communication and avoid temper displays themselves.[64]

How bipolar disorder and screen dependence are different		
ISSUE OR SYMPTOM	AS AN ASPECT OF BIPOLAR DISORDER	AS AN ASPECT OF SCREEN DEPENDENCE
Presence of tyrannical demeanor—does not accept the word no from parents and others.[65]	A core issue in early-onset bipolar disorder; probably reflects the child's sense that she or he lacks any control so he tries to assert complete control.	Expresses delusional arrogance and feels superior to all others because of gaming prowess; does not give parents moral authority to regulate behavior.
Extreme, destructive impulsivity.	Expresses mania (overwhelming, uncontrollable, and unfocused mental energy).	May result from chronic game conditioning to think fast without considering consequences.

How bipolar disorder and screen dependence are different (continued)

ISSUE OR SYMPTOM	AS AN ASPECT OF BIPOLAR DISORDER	AS AN ASPECT OF SCREEN DEPENDENCE
Late-evening mental and physical hyperactivity/sleep issues.	Related to documented circadian rhythm issues.	Nervous system is overstimulated by screen media use.
Presence of rage that is not reactive aggression to some real threat but comes out of nowhere.	Shows as a mixed state in children—depression expressed with manic force.	Expresses frustration with game play and depressive affect, which is a result of brain exhaustion due to chronic low-level stress and sleep deprivation.
Deceit and thievery (e.g., stealing credit cards).	Expresses mania and inability to see consequences or impact on others.	Driven by the need to acquire recreational screen media enhancements.
Self-mutilation, cutting, or suicidal.	Core issues in bipolar disorder; expresses powerful depressive state that is five times worse than depression in stand-alone cases.[66]	Not typically seen unless it is a theme in a violent video, which would be considered reenactment.
High anxiety.	Related to lack of a strong sense of self and an overexcited brain.	A result of brain exhaustion due to chronic low-level stress and sleep deprivation.

To distinguish screen dependence from bipolar disorder as a cause for issues, consider the following questions:[67]

- Has the child always had problems getting to sleep, even before he started gaming? Nighttime (usually around 9:00 p.m.) cognitive hyperactivity is often seen in children with bipolar disorder, and they often cannot get to sleep.

- Does the child experience rage that may come out of nowhere and last for over a half hour? Or, for older children, is he or she subject to frequent mood shifts or chronic irritability? Anger, which is expressed in meltdown, is different from rage that lasts more than a half hour and typically results in the child acting age regressed and beside himself with anger and aggressive affect. Rage is a sign of early-onset bipolar disorder.

- Is depression immobilizing or accompanied by psychotic phenomena, such as clinical paranoia, delusions, or hallucinations? Depression related to bipolar disorder is significantly more severe than depression related to screen dependence.

- Are there people in the child's immediate family who have been diagnosed with bipolar disorder, been hospitalized for any kind of psychiatric illness, or committed suicide? Bipolar disorder is highly inheritable, and there is a high likelihood of genetic transmission from grandparents to grandchildren or from parents to children.

- Is the child good at school but bad at home? For reasons specific to the disorder, most children who suffer from early-onset bipolar disorder are compliant and make the grade at school, but when they get home, all hell breaks loose. If this kind of "Jekyll and Hyde" persona exists, think bipolar disorder.

AUTISM SPECTRUM DISORDER (ASD)

ASD is a disorder of social communication that can gravely impair a child's social interactions. Autistic people cannot read others' facial expressions or nonverbal behavior. They cannot share others' interests in a group conversation and will break in with their own agenda. Also, they do not understand the unwritten rules of social conduct. Rules, norms, and personal expectations are part of the context, or field, within which social transactions take place. To the person with autism, every conversation is a new conversation; thus, much of the background information for the conversation is not held in awareness.[68]

The *DSM-IV* listed Asperger's syndrome (AS) as a milder subset of autism spectrum disorder. It was said to be different from ASD only in the fact that children with Asperger's syndrome do not have impairment in the use of language to achieve social goals early in their lives. In the author's experience, children with Asperger's syndrome have a marked advantage over children with a frank autistic condition in that they are much more capable of fitting in and learning to imitate the social behavior of neurotypical, or non-ASD, people.

- **Prevalence:** 1 to 2 percent in boys; 0.5 percent in girls.

- **Major challenges:** Loneliness is the major challenge for school-aged children with ASD, followed by severe difficulties with getting their needs met in social situations and being successful at school. Many children with ASD have the same executive function deficits as those with ADHD—severe inattention, distractibility, and difficulty being motivated to do anything that is not intrinsically interesting.[69] In addition, there are real problems with planning and initiating social and academic activities. The child appears lost in a world of his own. He may also be crippled by intense shyness, anxiety, obsessive thought patterns, and a predilection for frequent, loud, and disturbing meltdowns.

- **Typical school accommodations:** The Individuals with Disabilities Education Act (IDEA), a United States law, requires that ASD children be afforded a full range of special educational services. These could include assignment of a one-to-one aide at school as well as full-time placement in a special education classroom. If the child is placed in a general education environment (more typical for children with Asperger's syndrome), he may benefit from social skills training as well as specialized instruction in any subject matter that requires creative thinking or that is team based. Children on the autism spectrum may have a difficult time in any group-learning situation, as they typically have extremely poor listening skills and often misinterpret others' verbal and nonverbal behaviors and intentions or simply are oblivious to others' feelings.

- **Typical home accommodations:** The best home environment for children on the autism spectrum is extremely structured and predictable. There are rules for everything, including the child's morning routine, chores, homework routines, and getting to bed at night. ASD children tend to be exclusively visual and have severe problems following spoken sequences of instructions, so all rules must be visually posted, preferably in the kitchen and/or bedroom, and explained in detail, repetitively. Eventually the child learns the routine for himself and does not need prompting. Meltdowns should be expected when the child encounters frustration, and he should be taught methods for getting his needs met that eliminate the frustration that causes temper dyscontrol. Parents should not give in to the child as a result of a meltdown but should practice the demeanor of psychiatric hospital staff who look at temper fits as an attempt at communication and deal with it in a matter-of-fact manner.

How autism spectrum disorder and screen dependence are different

ISSUE OR SYMPTOM	AS AN ASPECT OF AUTISM SPECTRUM DISORDER	AS AN ASPECT OF SCREEN DEPENDENCE
Personal organization is absent; has appearance of being lost and disoriented.	A result of autistic tendency to hyperfocus and lack of ability to keep ongoing context in mind.	A result of executive function deficits related to chronic low-level brain stress from screen media use.
Meltdowns.	A result of frustration related to the inability to understand the environment and how to be resourceful.	A result of mood dysregulation caused by chronic low-level brain stress and exhaustion due to screen media use.
Inability to initiate and maintain social relationships.	A result of inability to listen and share attention in social situations.	Social anxiety related to chronic screen media use and loss of real friends.
Very poor ability to motivate and accomplish goals.	Cannot see benefits from any novel situation and has a need for sameness.	Brain reward circuits are dependent on screen media access, which are underactivated for anything else.
High anxiety.	Relates to the inability to understand others and meet requirements of the environment.	A result of chronic low-level brain stress and frustration caused by screen media use.

To distinguish screen dependence from an autism spectrum disorder as a cause for issues, consider the following questions:[70]

- Did the child use language to get social and emotional needs met from birth to age two or three? Did he or she ask for comforting or use language to give comfort to others? Autistic children do not do these things. They seem to be in their own world and do not have an emotional need for others.[71]

- Does the child understand the meaning of nonverbal behavior in others—what a frown or grin or a roll of the eyes means? Has the child shown empathy for other children? The brains of autistic children do not pay attention to the presence of others but tend to get absorbed only in their own interests.

- Is the child able to share attention with other children? Can he focus on a topic of conversation and follow it, or does he often jump in with irrelevant material? Coming in with unrelated material is typical of children with autism and Asperger's syndrome.

- Does the child understand the context, or setting, in a given situation? For example, does he know that he could privately tell his friend, another boy in his class, something personal about his body, but that he should not tell the whole class the same thing? The context is different. Autistic children do not take the physical or social context into account. They are *field independent*—to use a term borrowed from developmental psychology—they focus only on a figure in the foreground and do not take background into account.

LEARNING DISABILITIES (LD)

Children with learning disabilities have difficulty reading (dyslexia), writing (dysgraphia), or doing math (dyscalculia). These issues may be related to insufficient educational experience or to inherited impairments in memory, perception, mental processing, or output (writing and speaking). They may also be a result of an intellectual disability, which is shown in lower-than-average IQ scores.[72]

- **Prevalence:** 5 to 15 percent of children.

- **Major challenges:** Children with learning disabilities live with the shame of being behind their peers in one or more subjects at school. They often hide their inability to accomplish an academic task or take a failing grade and blame themselves rather than ask for help. Unfortunately, this population of children is greatly at risk of dropping out of school, and this risk can be seen as early as third grade in increasing absence from regular classes. The basic challenge these children face is the sense of futility that comes with trying as hard as they can to master a subject but failing to do so. If the problem is related to insufficient or inappropriate educational experience, there is a likelihood that screen dependence may be involved—the child pays attention only to his recreational screen media pursuits. Sleep deprivation may also cause learning deficits. It is important to know whether a learning disability is a result of an inherited impairment or screen dependence. If it is related to an onboard learning disability, such as dyslexia, or a psychiatric condition, such as ADHD (with its short-term memory deficits), parents need to choose a more complex remediation strategy and develop ways to work around learning problems rather than simply terminate excessive screen media access, which would be the most important order of business for a child with a screen dependence.

- **Typical school accommodations:** Learning disabilities are identified with the educational assessment used to set up the child's IEP and enroll him for special education services. Typically, the plan put together by special education staff at school will include one-to-one tutoring and special educational programming to help the child master academic skills so as to form a strong base for learning, retention, and accomplishment of educational and social milestones. The Individuals with Disabilities Education Act requires that special education departments provide a "free and appropriate education" in the **"least**

restrictive environment."[73] This means that school districts must use methods that permit a child to have a "normal as possible" school experience depending on his learning disability.

- **Typical home accommodations:** Again, there is the importance of predictability, structure, and routine for children with learning disabilities. Parents may choose to recruit specialized tutoring services. If tutoring is necessary to meet an IEP goal, the school district is responsible for carrying the cost. In many families with LD children, learning disabilities are seen in one or both biological parents. Often this can cause a problem because parents themselves do not recognize the issue in their children and resist remediation. These parents say things such as "We don't read books in this family," camouflaging the dyslexia in parents and the child, or "Her dad was horrible at math, too," camouflaging dyscalculia.

How learning disabilities and screen dependence are different		
ISSUE OR SYMPTOM	**AS AN ASPECT OF A LEARNING DISABILITY**	**AS AN ASPECT OF SCREEN DEPENDENCE**
Dyslexia.	Seen in the child's tendency to reverse position of letters and numbers and general difficulty in reading.	Caused by brain conditioning to process only rapidly received visual stimuli; reading ability does not develop because the child does not read.
Difficulty with any writing assignment along with inability to use punctuation correctly.	Result of inability to mentally compose written material or sound out words and the flow of sentences in the mind. Shows presence of dysgraphia.	Caused by underuse of brain centers tasked to write and read text-based material.

How learning disabilities and screen dependence are different (continued)

ISSUE OR SYMPTOM	AS AN ASPECT OF A LEARNING DISABILITY	AS AN ASPECT OF SCREEN DEPENDENCE
Poor spelling.	May be a result of memory issues typical of the ADHD and dyslexic population, along with poor word-attack skills—the child does not know how to sound out words.	Related to reliance on application-based spell-check features typical in the context of reading- and writing-avoidance behaviors.
Very poor keyboarding skills.	Has difficulty with hand-eye coordination but gets better with practice.	More accustomed to using game pads than keyboards; typing style is clumsy and inefficient; cannot touch-type.
Inability to compose correspondence or email.	Difficulty in structuring ideas; has ADHD, dyslexia, or visual-motor issues.	Has learned to text on a handheld device and composes emails that look like a text message.

To distinguish screen dependence from a learning disability as a cause for issues, consider the following questions:

- When did the child first start using screen media for recreation or as a teaching tool—in preschool, kindergarten, or later? There is very little evidence that programs such as *Baby Einstein* and other teaching applications result in improvement in the ability to apply knowledge in real situations or retain it after the medium is turned off. Several of the companies that promulgate these applications have been the subject of lawsuits for false representation of results.[74]

- Were learning disabilities specifically identified in the educational assessment part of the IEP? If no learning disabilities were identified and the child's IQ scores are at norm, suspect the presence of screen dependence.

- Does the child simply avoid homework or not turn in assignments? If a child is avoiding work related to a learning disability, it will typically be obvious what kind of specific impairment he is experiencing. If he simply rarely or never studies or turns in any homework, suspect screen dependence.

- Did the child show the presence of a specific learning disability or behavior evocative of a learning disability early in his life? If so, there is a strong possibility a learning disability is part of the picture.

- Is the child diagnosed with ADHD or an autism spectrum disorder? Each of these conditions comes with learning problems; if a child meets diagnostic criteria, these learning issues should be assessed and remediated, in addition to using strategies to reduce the amount of screen time.

The right solution is based on a correct understanding of the etiology of the issue

Knowing what the actual causes are of your child's lack of success at school and in his personal life is important. If there is an on-board psychiatric condition and treatment is available, you should make use of this treatment. If you do not, the untreated disorder may sabotage any attempts you make to write and enforce a screen control plan in your home.

There is another, equally important reason to get to know the true *etiology*—the medical term for *cause*—of your child's dysfunctional behavior and affect: Certain *psychiatric conditions are actually made worse* by too much recreational screen media use. These conditions include ADHD, anxiety issues, and bipolar disorder. If a child has one of these disorders in his makeup, compulsive screen media use is similar to taking a poison pill that makes his already distressing behavior worse. At present, there is no substantial longitudinal research on how long this effect lasts, but it is not unreasonable to assume that the damage may be long-term.

Early intervention is key. Once you know what is going on, you can take action in your home, at your child's school, and in conjunction with his medical providers so you can begin reversing any damage done. Emerging research from the field of neurogenesis points to the fact that the brain has amazing power to heal itself if the damage can be treated before a certain point in the child's life.

Your child may not be his brain's best friend! He is too young to know better. So you have to be that friend, doling out the tough love necessary to teach him how to control his screen dependence so he can accomplish cognitive tasks at home and at school that develop the full potential of his brain.

CHAPTER 4

The Deepest Wound: Interrupted Identity Development

In Chapter 1, we noted that chronic screen media use may cause delays in the physical development of the screen-dependent child. The look of weak muscularity in these children is often accompanied by a corresponding mental weakness, which is sensed by others as a lack of presence when they are around the child, as if he is only partially there mentally—playing the part but not really connecting with the audience.

The feeling of "pleasant but not present" is typical of children who have no sense of themselves as unique people with a distinctive set of gifts and strengths. Their sense of self-identity, or autobiography, has not developed because they have removed themselves from the real world and entered the artificial world of media. They are no longer quite in the present moment.

Identity development is a central requirement for success in life. If a child does not have a sense of self, he will experience clinically troubling delays in emotional and intellectual capacity and is at risk of developing mental illness, specifically depression and high anxiety.[75]

The search for identity is a lifelong quest. Your autobiography changes many times depending on your life circumstances and stage of emotional, intellectual, and moral development. But without this definite narrative, you cannot function in daily life; you cannot answer the three questions every human being encounters throughout a lifetime: Who am I? Who are all these others? What are we doing together?

Scholar Dr. Jean Houston calls this essential autobiography a person's **"great story."** She suggests that the story you tell yourself about you has the power to release your potential, integrate all aspects of yourself, and enable you to realize capabilities you did not know you possessed. Your sense of self is formed as you deal with frustration in life. Each challenge you face is a step in the formation of your identity. In meeting a challenge, or making mistakes in dealing with it, you write your own great story. First you meet the challenge, and then you remember that you met it. That is how you become the person you are.[76]

According to author and activist Ralph Nader, "Your best teacher is your last mistake"—a saying he learned from his father.[77] The wisdom of this statement runs contrary to the sentiment of many parents who believe they are doing the best job they can if they spare their children the pain of making mistakes. This often means sparing them the anxiety involved in taking on any task that challenges the priority they put on sedentary recreational screen media use. This *negative* great story of failure in life that comes with the reluctance to take risks can be as damaging to the psyches of children as can outright psychological abuse. A negative great story contains themes of personal victimhood, anger, and futility. These themes may be expressed as a self-fulfilling prophecy in the child's life.

Parents serve their children's well-being by helping them experience life in such a way that their identity will develop normally. Here we build on the work of developmental theorists, such as James Marcia, Robert Kegan, and Lawrence Kohlberg, to describe a process made up of six developmental stages that occur with some predictability.[78]

- **Stage One** occurs from birth to age two, or thereabouts. At this time, children find out from their family whether they are loved. If children get the right experience, they proceed into life believing that they belong there and the universe is friendly. This learning forms the bedrock for the development of children's identity as progression through the next five stages occurs.

- **Stage Two** occurs from age two to age five, or so. At this time, children learn that they have power, efficacy, and the ability to get needs met. They learn the power of saying "no." Success in negotiating this stage has a lot to do with parents' ability to withstand the challenge of their child's will and stay lovingly in power. A child has to be able to put his foot down and know his parents will not abandon him, hurt him, or shame him for expressing his will.

- **Stage Three** occurs during elementary school, ages six through twelve. This time is a transition from fantasy and free-form play to group games and sports. During the school-age stage, children begin feeling guilty over wrong choices. They learn rules of how to relate to others, as well as rules of exclusion and inclusion. They learn to express emotions, beginning with learning how to share and keep secrets. Between the ages of seven and nine, children become more aware of their private thoughts and feelings and begin to compare themselves with peers.

- **Stage Four** occurs in middle school, sometime after the age of ten and before the age of thirteen. At Stage Four, children begin to define who they will be in adolescence. At this point they enact all the good things and the not-so-good things they have learned up to this point. Children experience a powerful pull toward their peer group and away from their parents. They begin firming up, in a formal way, their sense of who they are and express, "I am this, not that, and these are my friends."

- **Stage Five** occurs from the beginning of puberty, around age thirteen, through the formal end of adolescence, at around age nineteen, when adolescents step out into the world and try their hand at adult themes, relationships, the world of work, and increasingly complex educational involvement. They solidify their peer group and identify strongly with it. The adolescent's autobiography becomes a blend of his feelings and beliefs about his own capabilities with the values he absorbs from his peer and friendship groups. All the learning he has experienced for good and for not so good becomes part of his sense of identity at this time.

- **Stage Six** includes the years between the ages of eighteen or nineteen and the mid-twenties. Most young adults experience disturbance of mind and spirit at this time. Typically, young adults say they know that there is something they should be doing but they do not know what it is. This is the time when young men and women go looking for their life's work. They enter a phase in their lives in which they gather up everything they have learned and hit some big challenge with it, such as finding a job, finding a vocation, pursuing their education, and/or finding something they love to do and want to learn more about.

If, at Stage Six, the young adult has the good fortune to have successfully negotiated the joys and sorrows of emotional development in adolescence and early adulthood, he may experience the powerful pull of imagination and intuition in a particular direction. This would be the little voice in the ear called *vocatus* in Latin, which says, "You have this particular talent, and the world needs this talent right now."

Or, if negotiation is not successful, the young adult may experience an *identity crisis:* This is felt as great tension and discontent in the psyche resulting from the person being pulled away from the ways of his past by forces from his future. Some youth attempt to resolve the crisis by using their parents' lives and values as lodestones for adulation or repulsion, that is, they adopt or reject their parents' values wholesale. Or they may put the identity project in *moratorium* and keep living day-to-day, putting off the decision and going along with circumstance. Moratorium can last for years.[79]

Identity development continues for the rest of a person's life. If a young adult has a solid developmental foundation, it is possible for him to now experience *intuitive knowing* about the kind of work and lifestyle that would bring him meaning. If he has successfully consolidated a sense of identity, he appears more himself, confident, and optimistic. People get a sense of presence when he is around. They feel like they are in the presence of a person who "knows who he is."

Identity and screen overuse

So, what does all of this have to do with screen overuse? Looking at our clients' lives, we see that too much screen media use stunts a child's physical, emotional, cognitive, and spiritual development. In the same way that smoking cigarettes can stunt a person's growth, spending too much time with recreational screen media can freeze a person in time developmentally. This spiritual, emotional, and cognitive "failure to thrive" syndrome manifests differently depending on when the screen media overuse starts, but *the core injury always occurs to the child's sense of identity.*

A person's identity develops as a result of facing and mastering the frustrations and challenges encountered in life. Screen media overuse orients the child away from reality in such a way that ordinary daily challenges, such as dealing successfully with uninteresting schoolwork, do not happen along with the potential learning that could occur from dealing with these challenges. This results in impairment in the brain's cognitive and emotional processing structures that are used to solve problems in both the social and academic domains. Brain executive function and social confidence are the primary casualties. The child feels so overwhelmed outside the comfort of his darkened room that he cannot cope with ordinary stress and learn from it.[80]

The effects of screen dependence at each stage of development

We observe that overuse of recreational screen media slams the door on the opportunities provided by real life for identity development from two directions: it works to keep these predicaments away from the child, and if he does come into contact with them, it prevents him from being able to absorb and integrate what these challenges have to teach him. The following sections detail how screen dependence causes damage at each of the six stages of identity development.

STAGE ONE

If a child is introduced to screen media at, say, age two with electronic games, for whatever purpose, the medium will be more interesting than the silly peek-a-boo games or inane baby noises of adult caregivers. The flickering lights, curious noises, and immediate reinforcement of the device nullifies the toddler's interest in anything less dramatic. Who cares about animals, science, fun books, and other kids when *Baby Einstein* is so much fun to be with!

Giving a child screen media at this time may cause a break in his contact with his mother and other important people in his life. It may also limit his exposure to basic sensory information sources, such as the smell of backyard flowers, the feel of grass under his feet, and the sensation of rain in his hair and on his skin. If he gets hooked on a digital device, there will not be much exploration or contact with the world around him. Without this contact, the child's basic sense of confidence in his ability to soothe himself and deal with frustrations he encounters are diminished. He does not have enough of the kind of experience that must be present for identity development to take place.[81]

Leaving a child with *Baby Einstein* for long stretches of time is not good for his brain—great as a babysitter but horrible for brain development and identity formation.

STAGE TWO

This is the stage when a child learns the fundamentals of assertiveness: the ability to state personal needs and understand that the stating of those needs, wants, and demands to parents does not result in loss of their love. In terms of identity development, children find themselves in a push-and-pull struggle for power with their parents.

Once dependence on screen media is established, parents gain an ideal babysitter. No longer do they have to deal with a child's complaints about being bored. They do not have to deal with their child having an argument with his friend or nemesis who lives next door. Parents get along fine with the child as long as they put no limitations on screen media access. Unfortunately, the price the child pays for this arrangement is in his failure to develop the ability to craft give-and-take solutions to problems with others, which results in structures essential for social adaptation not forming normally and not becoming part of the child's repertoire of strength—his identity.

Eventually, a power struggle over the child's increasing dependence on screen media use to the exclusion of everything else in life may cause parents to limit screen media access. At this time, the child may threaten violence to himself or others—remember, he has no skill set for peaceful negotiation of his needs. This struggle may result in a deepening emotional rift with the child's parents, who lose a sense of attachment to him and come to see him as a nuisance.

If overuse of screen media occurs at this stage, the child will not develop the ability to negotiate power struggles, and he will incur wounds to his self-esteem because of his parents' angry alienation from him. Though he will fight hard for his screen media use, the conflict with parents will take its toll in terms of his self-esteem. Though he may win, at some level he will be disgusted with himself.

STAGE THREE

The changes children go through in first through fifth grades are foundational for the rest of their lives. This time marks a child's initiation into his social group and the evolution of his psyche to self-awareness, self-valuing, and moral development. The child who successfully navigates this stage shows the presence of well-developed social skills, including the ability to deal gracefully with social rejection.

Thomas Lewis and his coauthors write in their book *A General Theory of Love* about a phenomenon they term **limbic resonance.**[82] This is the experience of emotional sharing between people in each other's physical presence that enables each person to change and grow as a result of their mutual emotional connection. Limbic resonance does not occur in the virtual world between people who have no physical connection and are only texting or talking to each other through digital media. Thus, when children discuss their online friendships, they are more accurately describing a connection with fellow machine operators who really know nothing about each other except the fact that all enjoy a particular game or medium.

If the child orients too much toward sedentary screen media at this developmental stage, he does not gain the experience to develop the sophisticated social abilities required of children in our increasingly complex society.[83] He becomes bound to his computer and interacts with others mainly through screen media. He does not experience the development of limbic resonance along with its powerful impact on the development of his capability for social complexity and its contribution to the development of his identity. Without cultivation of the ability for limbic resonance, the child's emotional and social development is retarded.

In this vein, direct interpersonal interaction with other children and adults is required if the child is going to develop *social confidence*. If he does not experience the requisite social interaction, he may become socially anxious or socially aggressive. He will find it very difficult to fit in except with groups of other gamer kids who talk about video games and other screen media.[84]

For the screen-dependent child, the natural impulse to socialize with peers is diluted through social media. Unfortunately for the child, human beings need direct contact with other humans to develop normally, and the brain does not recognize text messages or flickering images on a screen as direct contact. The child is starving himself psychologically and emotionally. People grow as a result of their relationships. The screen-dependent child does not grow to full potential because of the lack of social contact that is needed for development.

Social media do not provide the experience needed to develop social identity because they lack the give-and-take that occurs in face-to-face conversation with other children through which this identity develops. The alienation from others that occurs at this point begins to show in the child's personality as *social anxiety*. Desperately trying to satisfy his psyche's natural need for real peer contact at this time in his life, but lacking the in-person experiences to do so, he becomes highly dependent on the opinions of others he meets online. And with this dependence comes a vulnerability to being bullied. This is a recipe for the development of depression and more severe mental illness.[85] More about the specific effects of chronic social media dependence on the development of children's personalities will be discussed in the next chapter.

STAGE FOUR

Children go through a major shift in identity around the time of middle school. At about the age of twelve, a child begins to wrestle with the issue of adolescent identity. He observes other children and starts making choices and decisions about his personal values, dress, preference for music, and gender identity. If he becomes screen dependent at this time, his capability to move away from the familiar precincts of his supportive fifth-grade class and into the rough-and-tumble of middle school will be compromised. He will not have the social skills, self-confidence, and cognitive skills to claim his place among his soon-to-be-adolescent peers. Screen-dependent children in middle school may experience a powerful loneliness and confusion due to the lack of identity development. Once again, their only community will be other gamer kids whom they will call friends but who are really fellow machine operators talking to each other over headsets, mostly in the middle of the night.

The most obvious damage in terms of identity development is noticed as a kind of profound mental laziness, a penchant for taking the easy way out, always along with avoidance of any risk and activity that takes the child away from screen media. Many children who are screen dependent at this time in their lives also show a disinterest in competing with others in athletics or academics.[86]

If chronic screen dependence keeps the child out of contact with others during this developmental stage, he may remain fixed at the middle-school emotional age well into middle adolescence. Once again, parents will report that he seems much younger emotionally than other kids his age.

Children trapped into screen dependence at Stage Four may either experience a deepening of depression or anxiety or fake the symptoms of these psychiatric diagnoses to take parents' attention off screen media use and compel them to permit more use. Many parents attempt to soothe a disturbed and unhappy child by permitting more screen media use, or they allow him to stay home from school because he seems so unhappy. Of course, when he is home he is interacting with screen media all day long. Either decision made by parents is the wrong remedy for their child.

STAGE FIVE

If a child is screen dependent at Stage Five, there is a greater probability that his psychiatric symptoms will worsen to the point of impairing function in daily life. He will be diagnosed with depression or an anxiety disorder. Traditional teen interests involving distancing from parents and relating to peers will not be evident. If the child is a male, he will not want to stray too far from home. He will become apathetic, ill tempered, and demanding. Screen-dependent girls may resist going to school and deploy a myriad of manipulative strategies aimed at preventing parental interference with their screen media use. Girls are especially at risk of developing depression and anxiety disorders as a result of compulsive use of social media. What caregivers may not know is that a girl is doing something—becoming screen dependent—that actively worsens psychiatric issues.

Adolescence is a time of intense physical development, but screen-dependent boys do not move their bodies, so they become either obese or underweight as a result of eating junk food or chronic undereating. They begin to suffer from weakness syndrome, and their bodies appear weak and unsupported by normal muscle tone. Also, inactivity may contribute to the development of diabetes and other conditions related to an intensely sedentary lifestyle. Now the child includes a sense of personal failure in his great story because he cannot keep himself healthy or physically strong.

In terms of identity formation for the screen-dependent adolescent, the all-important identity crisis that typically occurs around age eighteen is put on hold. The child neither forecloses on his parents' values nor rejects these values. He does not develop a personal sense of identity because, as a result of chronic screen dependence, he does not have the repertoire of learning experience behind him to make decisions about self-concept. The screen-dependent child in Stage Five may float from one interest to another, one fad video game or media challenge to another, never really having a sense of himself as a person in any of it.[87]

STAGE SIX

Developmentally, the human psyche seeks a rite of passage at Stage Six. This is the process of successfully meeting a challenge or sequence of challenges so novel that a person has no onboard skill set for dealing with them. To transcend the situation, he must pull strength, skill, and capability out of himself that he did not know he possessed, and his life changes permanently as a result. If the person is successful, he achieves a new sense of identity, but first he has to go through the rite before he can incorporate what he learns into his great story.

The psyche requires the rite of passage just as lungs require air. The problem is that if a particular challenge is perceived to be too painful, the challenge will be avoided. If the child has been screen dependent to this point, he will instinctively avoid any novel situation that could bring pain. Unfortunately for him, this stage requires a lot of courage, and if this courage has been undermined by chronic screen media use for the past ten years or so, the child will not be able to experience the rite of passage. He will have very low self-confidence and feel unable to make even the simplest decisions about what to do.

This impact on self-esteem is evident in the dozens of young adults in clinical practice who have complained that their parents continue to foster their **learned helplessness.** Although parents may allow them to play video games all night and provide all the amenities of a comfortable life well into their twenties, these young adults are angry. And they are depressed, and should be. They have allowed their parents and their own surrender to the pull of gaming to steal the challenges and troubles they need to learn about life.

Clever media companies provide false rites of passage

The companies that promulgate screen media are cognizant of the psyche's need for a rite of passage, and they give adolescents and young adults a false experience of it. A close look at video game themes reveals that most games are fashioned around heroic rites of passage that give players a virtual experience of meeting and transcending some important challenge. But this is not a genuine rite of passage, and the superficially arrogant manner that gamers assume when they play well does not indicate that they have graduated into adulthood. In a genuine rite of passage, they would be required to dig into their own resources, their own repertoire of skills or raw intuition, to survive a real challenge in the real world. In the false rite of passage of the video game world, the gamer simply has to play long enough to learn the secret maneuver that is required to get to the next level.

Unfortunately, video game themes often succeed at tricking young adults into believing that somehow success at the game means something about success in life. It does not. In the gamer's real life, out of his room, out in the world, nothing is happening. It may take years for him to have the insight to know what he has done to himself.

Identity development paces moral development

We suggest that screen dependence keeps a child forever young emotionally and cognitively. In terms of growing up, there is equally important damage in the domain of *moral development*. If an addictive practice deforms the morality in a culture, it deforms the way people treat each other. History shows us that when practical morality devolves in a culture, the culture cannot survive.

Identity formation and moral development pace each other. If you know who you are, you automatically have a set of criteria for the decisions you make and the way you treat others. If you do not know who you are, you most likely will accept any version of the truth that is delivered by someone or something that you trust, but that source may not be trustworthy in the least. The erosion of the screen-dependent child's ability to think critically has an impact on her or his ability to think morally and make decisions about how to treat other people.

We agree with Dr. Lawrence Kohlberg, a pioneer in the field of human moral development, that people do go through predictable stages of development in their sense of social empathy and morality that paces identity development.[88] According to Kohlberg, very young children make the right decisions because they fear rejection or punishment by their parents. In elementary school, children do the right thing because they want others to like them. By middle school they become rule-bound and seek to have others treat them fairly. Later, as their character mature, their motivation for moral behavior may become a deep desire for civility; they do the right thing because they feel a sense of interdependence with others.

Finally, at the highest level of moral development, adolescents and young adults start following their own internal sense of right and wrong. They discover their own inner voice and are no longer bound to make decisions based on social fear, reward, or punishment. It is not difficult to recognize people who are living their life at this level. They are typically comfortable with themselves, take responsibility for their actions, and tell the truth. They are what the aboriginals would call "initiated." You trust them to make the morally right decision. You trust their character.

Many screen-dependent children do not reach Kohlberg's last stage of moral development. It is not that recreational screen media overuse makes them violent, but screen media overuse keeps them stuck way below their potential for being civil, responsible, and empathetic.

If a child is getting good grades, why limit her or his recreational screen media use?

Some of the children whom we serve in our practices are very screen dependent but are still earning acceptable grades. In this situation, should parents back off on their attempts to put limits on recreational screen media use? We would advise parents not to cut back on controls simply because a child is doing okay at school. To do so suggests that school is the most important part of the child's identity development. School success is obviously important to the child's sense of success in her or his life, but it is only part of the picture.

The public school system in the United States is remarkably flawed in its ability to actually educate children. Periodic performance testing and the number of graduates who go to college are not accurate measures. The importance of the public school system can be found in its *potential* to draw out a child's talents and provide a venue for the development of a sound social identity—a sense of who the child is in the context of her or his peer group, including strengths and challenges in social settings.

School is important for identity development because it provides a venue for a child to challenge her or his own disinterest or lack of capability in a knowledge area and transcend these challenges in order to change her or his concept of self—"I didn't think I could do it, but I did. This is who I am!" The school setting is central to the child's development of social identity because it is where a child learns to get along and get her or his needs met with other people who may be different in terms of race, culture, and intellectual ability. But succeeding at school is not, in itself, essential to identity development. What is essential is that the child is afforded the opportunity to face and transcend cognitive, physical, emotional, and social challenges in her or his life, and this requires that the child actually get out into the real world. School is part of that real world, but only part of it.

Compulsive use of recreational and social screen media can be so destructive because it prevents children from engaging in life, dealing with unpleasantness, and learning from the process. When a child is lonely, she or he needs to feel lonely and learn how to reach out to make and keep friends. When a child is resentful from having to perform chores, she or he needs to *feel* the resentment and deal with it. When a child's body and brain are screaming for fresh air and exercise, the child needs to obey these demands and get out there and move.

And when the child is bored, she or he needs to figure out how to deal with it. We talk a lot in this book about how parents feel it is their job to rescue their children from the experience of intense emotional states, including boredom. For screen-dependent children, *everything* except recreational screen media is boring. Boredom is the fertile soil from which imagination grows. Yes, it is painful and it is difficult for parents to see their children in pain. But it is necessary pain, and dealing with it pushes children into endeavors they would never have imagined. This is far different from pressing the "on" button on their digital device.

Learning who we are from pain

In the movie *Unbroken,* the audience learns the story of Louis Zamperini, an American Olympic athlete turned airman during World War II who was captured and tortured in a Japanese prison camp. Zamperini survived the ordeal and vowed to hunt down and kill the commandant of the camp who had tortured him. As it turned out, he did locate the commandant some ten years after the war ended, but instead of killing him, he forgave him.[89]

Zamperini's story illustrates how one's personal identity is formed while dealing with pain, be it emotional pain or physical suffering. At the end of this ordeal, Zamperini could well have described his personal identity in this way: My life holds the will and strength to survive the greatest torments the world can inflict on a person. I am a person who does not pollute my life energy with hatred. In the case of children seeking to find themselves post–screen dependence, as with Zamperini, their identity can be defined by knowing about unseen talents within their psyche that come to the forefront when the going gets tough.

This principle presents itself in the lives of many young clients. One boy, named Mark, is a bright fifteen-year-old with a severe case of Tourette's syndrome (TS). As a result of his TS, Mark had a vocal tic, which was a semivoluntary vocalization that he felt compelled to make every ten minutes or so in the form of a loud shriek. This tic resulted in his isolation at school and rejection by many students.

One day a teacher asked Mark to write a page in response to the question, "Who am I?" His result was as follows: "I am he who gets up off the ground at the end of the school day and brushes off all the shame, humiliation, and pain I experience from TS to go to school the next day. I am he who keeps on going to school despite this torment."

On that day, Mark taught an unforgettable lesson about identity formation: The quickest route for a person to discover her or his true nature is to remember when pain has been transcended, and, using that memory, list the talents, characteristics, and energies that got her or him through the ordeal. This is a description of the core self, the essential energy, and essential nature of the person.

You could say that personal identity is sensed between the terror and the triumph. On the one hand is the terror that comes with severe pain. On the other hand is the event of moving through it to discover one is still alive. A person's great story is changed by this event.

How to help a child develop a positive "great story" from the pain of withdrawal

The pain a child goes through during withdrawal from screen dependence can provide valuable insight about her or his strength and other wisdom related to the child's great story. The following is a short verbal exercise that may provide a teaching moment to this effect. Some insight is required to complete the exercise, so most children would have to be in their teens to learn from it. The interaction described here does not have to be accomplished in any particular order.

This conversation should take place in a comfortable setting where your child feels safe. The first thing to do is make clear that you see what she or he is going through and respect your child for having the strength to endure. There should be no hint of parental advice-giving. The best place might be during a walk or at a café. Open the discussion with some note of the Zamperini story or a story from your own life that was a rite of passage for you toward your own maturity and compassion. Then ask your child to describe some difficult personal moment when she or he felt overwhelmed by the situation but *somehow made it through*. Guide the discussion by asking questions, such as the following:

- What ordeal did you experience and transcend? It could have been as mild as learning to ride a bicycle or as serious as dealing with the death of a parent or friend.

- What pain or heartbreak comes to mind when you think about this event?

- What did you do to deal with this ordeal? Specifically, how did you get through it? What talents did you deploy? What kind of fear did you struggle with in this situation that eventually had to be dealt with in some way? What strengths of character were revealed? What vulnerabilities were revealed?

Now ask your child to express her or his insight in a sentence that begins with "I am a being who" or "I am a person who." Encourage her or him to try to self-describe this insight as "in process" rather than "arrived," for example, "I am a loving person who chooses love over hatred even in the darkest times; I am a being who is in the process of learning to love; I am a person who is living the process of knowing my own truth." If your child gets stuck and cannot generalize the experience of the ordeal to identify personal strengths, suggest some positive features you draw from the narrative about your child's identity, strengths, and challenges. It is important not to push for any particular outcome but to actively listen to your child as she or he struggles with the task of self-definition. This is how a great story is built—one ordeal at a time, one success at a time.

Wisdom from Rainer Maria Rilke

The German poet Rainer Maria Rilke shares great wisdom in his poem "The Man Watching," which discusses the life of children and what they need for their development.[90] The poet tells us that, as was the case with Louis Zamperini, the most important thing in life is to continually engage the struggle to stay alive, focused, and in contact with the world. The important thing is not to give up.

In a similar fashion, it is not a stretch to say that the development of one's personal, social, and moral identity is a process through which a child comes to see himself as an originator of his own behavior, captain of his own ship. It is a process of losing one's sense of victimhood. Children who recover from screen dependence typically do so because they feel better about themselves for each and every little victory involved in returning to the world, the real world. Error acceptance is the bottom line, and they understand that everyone makes mistakes. So the question must be what have they learned? Learning is how a child forms her or his own great story by struggling, hurting, daring to love, and making mistakes, and by building a magnificent great story, one risk at a time.

A Tale of Two Boys

by Cynthia

Alex is six years old. Josh is also six years old. Both boys are starting first grade. Both have involved parents who express concern for their child's academic progress and individual growth. Both have met appropriate physical milestones and appear cognitively bright. The similarities begin to fade, and I feel a sense of sadness as I continue my narrative.

Josh is giggly about gaming but cannot write the alphabet in order. Reading is of little interest and extremely difficult. Math and telling time make no sense and are pretty much unimportant. Josh is highly distracted and not quite present in most tutoring sessions, unless he flips the subject to his video gaming. He recently announced to me—with all sincerity—that he was going to "drop out of school and just have fun for the rest of his life." He finds school "very boring." He would prefer to "play video games all day." Josh's imagination, innocence, and sense of wonder are being rapidly stripped from his identity.

Josh stays up until midnight the majority of school nights watching screens, and my yawn-o-meter clocks him at fifteen yawns per hour during most tutoring sessions. He is sleep deprived. He is afraid of the unknown. When the FedEx man delivered a package to the porch, he seriously wondered if it was a bomb. Josh is intent on the idea of wanting to buy and sell people as a result of hundreds of hours of playing *Clash of Clans*. As I departed one session, Josh was standing on his deck overlooking the family's backyard. In his hands, braced against a wicker chair, was a real crossbow—the kind used in archery contests. He had announced earlier that week that he wanted to kill an animal. Josh doesn't know it yet, but *he* is the one who has been bought . . . by a gaming company.

Don't get me wrong. Parenting is both tough and delightful. Parents do the best they can with the information they have at the time. This is the first generation of parents to raise children under the gaming cloud. No easy task. Once parents are awakened from the trance, things change. Josh's mother is concerned about his behavior. She knows staying up late and playing *Clash of Clans* and other games have not resulted in positive outcomes. She does not feel in charge. She has not yet awakened.

On the other hand, Alex is delighted with learning about the world and has a keen sense of wonder. He is reading at a second-grade level and loves the magic of it. He can clearly understand analog time down to the minute and exhibits great self-confidence in his ability to solve addition and subtraction problems using two digits. He laughs easily and appropriately. His innocence is intact.

Alex clearly gets an appropriate amount of sleep, according to my yawn-o-meter. He is also thrilled by Santa Claus and disappointed that I do not know everything. Adults should know EVERYTHING! He is in awe of school and being around his friends. His imagination is enhanced by the outdoors, whether watching a neighborhood ground squirrel gather leaves for winter or a red-headed woodpecker drill holes into a backyard tree. Alex recently found out there was no Tooth Fairy and asked me not to tell his younger brother. He was shocked when he discovered one of his friends told a lie. He is developing a sense of empathy and morality.

Alex is beyond thrilled with learning and having fun while learning. Every new book is an opportunity for investigative questions: "How long after a shark loses a tooth will it grow another one? Why do cats meow?" Alex does not play video games. Never has.

CHAPTER 5

The Gangster, the Golem, and the Charmer: How Becoming Screen Dependent Changes a Child's Personality

Screen-dependent children use manipulative strategies, threats, and dishonesty to ensure access to their preferred screen media. It makes sense that screen dependence causes a child to display primitive behavior because the dependence possesses the fear button in his brain—a structure deep within the limbic (instinctual) brain region. Once this button is pushed, it sends out a master command to the cortical (thinking) brain to counter the threat. Although the dependent pattern lives in the limbic brain, it possesses the power to take over the cortical brain with all its functional intelligence and make that brain do its bidding. In a manner of speaking, the screen dependence "zombifies" the child with the terror that he may lose access if he lets down his guard for a minute.[91]

The screen-dependent child must always be seeking access even if he is pretending to be interested in other things. As is the case for those with chemical dependencies, the child's personality morphs to incorporate a set of favorite tools he uses to control people around him, exemplifying three dominant patterns in the way children encode manipulative strategies into their everyday behavior: the Gangster, the Golem, and the Charmer.

The Gangster

The previous chapter described how screen dependence stunts the growth of identity and moral development. Although this practice may damage a child's brain, playing video games for normal children, even deeply screen-dependent normal children, does not transform these children into psychopaths—a condition diagnosed as **antisocial personality disorder** by psychiatrists in the *DSM-5*.[92] This being said, many screen-dependent children will use a manipulative tool kit that resembles one used by people with antisocial personality disorder. Gangster behavior includes

- chronic irritability, with a tendency to go off at a moment's notice along with behavioral surliness—the child will, for example, refuse to talk to parents or will favor them with a few words to get something he wants from them;

- frustration intolerance;

- a tendency to blame others for all of his issues;

- a lack of remorse or concern for what his behavior is doing to his family and a lack of empathy for others experiencing the suffering he may cause;

- chronic lying;

- use of obscenity;

- a persistent attitude of irresponsibility and disregard for any obligation to his parents or himself to accomplish homework or chores;

- an incapacity to maintain and nurture enduring relationships;

- a loss of a sense of conscience—not completely, as in the case of a genuine psychopath, but situationally, as when, for example, he misrepresents his parents as approving of his online purchases on one of their credit cards.

These are the traits of the Gangster personality type, which is directly emulated in heroic terms in the game *Grand Theft Auto 5*. The Gangster is the most aggressive of the three types of screen-dependent children described in this chapter. Our client research suggests that this child is also most likely to be diagnosed with psychiatric issues involving conduct disorder and violent behavior.

The Golem

Another variation of behavior can be seen in the Golem personality type. True to the roots of the golem legend in ancient Hebrew stories, the child starts looking like he is "being made out of inanimate matter"—think of the character of Gollum in *The Lord of the Rings*.[93] The Golem is a true slave to his craving and made very weak by it. Golem behavior manifests in

- a tendency to whine and collapse in the face of any difficult challenge;

- a loss of muscle tension—the child looks weak and has underdeveloped muscle tone and coordination;

- body mass abnormalities—he is either too thin or too fat for his age;

- presence of two psychiatric diagnoses: depression and anxiety. In a withdrawn state, he may refuse to talk with anyone, leaving parents painfully in the dark about what is going on with him;

- chronic sleep deprivation along with the problems it causes, including inattention and distractibility;

- very poor social confidence—the child acts socially and sexually immature;

- lack of development of basic skills or knowledge at school—his educational level is significantly below his actual age.

We observe that children who inhabit the Golem personality type are most likely to have parents who feel guilty for the child's condition, so they grant greater access to screen media as a result of this guilt.

The Charmer

Then, there is the Charmer. This type of screen-dependent child does not raise his voice in anger, as does the Gangster, or pout and wince, as does the Golem. He gets his way with persuasion. The Charmer knows how to tell people what they want to hear. Core features of the Charmer are

- having a *false presence*—he says the right things, but you never really get a sense of who he is or what he cares about;

- earning grades at school that are somewhat appropriate for his skill set and IQ, but you get the sense he could do much better if school were more important to him. Or, he may be failing several classes. Either way, there is no guilt;

- showing chronic sleep deprivation and the overall presentation of weakness, as is the case with the Golem;

- having difficulty in nurturing and maintaining enduring relationships;

- suffering from mild *anhedonia*—nothing really makes him happy (except screen media use).

The Charmer is the cleverest of the three types. He avoids the direct attack approach of the Gangster or the severely impaired presentation of the Golem, preferring to find ways to please whomever he is dealing with in order to continue his level of screen media use. If parents complain that he is doing nothing worthwhile with his life, he may get a little job that does not take too much time out of his day and do that job to make them happy so they can say, "At least he is moving forward with something in his life." If parents are concerned about grades, the Charmer will put in just enough effort at school to move his Ds and Fs to Cs and Ds and will reduce his missing assignments from thirty-one to seventeen.

As with the other two types, the Charmer, when he is not doing something to meet the basic requirements of his parents or teachers, is accessing his favorite game, watching YouTube, or watching others play online. He rarely has friends over unless it is to game, and that is what he does at their houses. Most significantly, the Charmer is apathetic about his future. Although he may be somewhat unrealistic, even grandiose, about his future, he does not have the ambition to do anything, really, except use recreational screen media as much, and as often, as possible.

The unifying theme of all three of the screen-dependent personalities is a *lack of personal imagination*. Although the child may ardently insist that screen media use builds his creative imagination, the process of getting through his game involves simply repeating steps to get to a higher level—being an efficient operant learner in the same way animals are trained to perform a task by conditioning and reinforcement. He is not exercising his imagination but is *reflecting the imagination* of the corporations that devised the game or created the YouTube media.

From Charmer to Gangster—the impact of social media

Around the beginning of grade school, at Developmental Stage Three, children go through a powerful impulse to connect socially with other children. In the best case, children are able to locate themselves within a social network that nurtures the evolving need for connection outside the child's immediate family. At this age, some children develop friendships that will last a lifetime. A signatory pattern of these friendships is limbic resonance, which is the brain's experience of empathy. It is listening to another person from the heart.

Limbic resonance is seen in a child's expression of any emotional state, be it awe, delight, anger, love, sadness, fear, hurt, resentment, or appreciation. When this type of communication occurs, the brain changes itself to accommodate the new information and makes it part of the child's self-definition of who she or he is. This is how social identity develops and identity itself forms—from both minor and major experiences of limbic resonance with others.

Often we hear of a child who develops a friendship with another child who, when she or he first appeared in the child's life, was the child's archnemesis. The relationship may have started in anger and hurt but, for some reason, morphed into a deep and enduring friendship. The personal identity of both of these children changes through the process of transcending mutual antagonism to arrive at friendship. Each child now has awareness—without knowing the psychological terms—of how *perception* and *circumstance* can impact people in relationships and, perhaps, how important forgiveness is for achieving deep connection with others.

There is an old belief that play is a child's work. In play, children enact dilemmas and predicaments they are facing in their lives. The dialogue of play occurs in limbic resonance with other children, and it is this interaction that enables each child to resolve the issues she or he faces in life. All of this is to say that the development of personal identity requires a great deal of face-to-face interaction between people. If this face-to-face interaction does not occur, identity development will be retarded.

How does the presence of cell phones, texting, and social media play into this dynamic process? Children today are the first generation raised on social media. Our client research informs us that if a child in grade school is given a cell phone, her or his process of identity development will *immediately* go to half speed, pulled back exactly by the amount of time spent using the cell phone to text others or use social or recreational media. It does not matter whom she or he is texting. If the child is not present in face-to-face communication, her or his brain will not develop at the same rate as would that of a child who does not use digital media.

In the book *Reclaiming the Conversation: The Power of Talk in a Digital Age*, Dr. Sherry Turkle cites research to suggest that having a cell phone in the presence of conversation limits the possibility of empathetic communication and of identity formation and moral development in children and young adults.[94] She details this process from her observations of college students and states that empathetic communication requires tolerance for silence and patience. In any conversation there may be small talk at the beginning, but if discussants have the patience to keep listening, they may find, quite quickly, that their interaction becomes genuinely interesting.

Turkle asserts that lack of patience and intolerance for the messy emotionality and ambiguity of face-to-face conversation is made worse by the availability of cell phones. Now, instead of doing a little bit of muscling through the listening process, children grab their cell phones to discern whether someone who is really interesting wants their attention. This behavior, Turkle concludes, is specific to a generation brought up to believe that you can get an instant response if you have the right app.[95]

Upon further examination of this dynamic, it becomes clear that the universal presence of cell phones greatly inhibits the development of emotional intimacy between children and is toxic to the growth of personal identity. In our client population, we observe that other effects spring from this identity retardation. First, lacking a sense of self, children turn to others, anyone, online for affirmation and become obsessed with being admired or seen as powerful by other social media users. This may cause them to articulate a split social personality: they may be friendly and likeable in person, inhabiting the Charmer personality style, but once they get on their device and into social media, they devolve into the Gangster personality and become tyrannical, foul-mouthed bullies. In the twisted, rootless milieu of the Internet, this kind of behavior is a sign of strength and dominance, qualities that many children find attractive.[96]

The term *rescue triangle* refers to a pattern of interaction often seen in families in which family members alternate among being each other's persecutors, rescuers, or victims. In fact, this is a common pattern seen in many social environments and is not particular to families with screen-dependency issues. Rescue triangles develop when people do not want to accept responsibility for their own behavior and get into blaming others for causing them to behave badly. It is not uncommon in family therapy to see siblings alternate between being each other's victims and persecutors, depending on the issue.

Children who compulsively use social media for a sense of well-being often enact the rescue triangle with each other. They may persecute and bully one child online while being bullied by another. Or they may form alliances and go into rescuer mode with each other. The persecutor, victim, and rescuer ego states roughly correspond to the Gangster, the Golem, and the Charmer personality types seen in families with children who are heavily screen dependent, and children's social identity development is twisted into a parody of normal identity development by the presence of social media.

Three common markers of screen dependence: apathy, ignorance, and arrogance

When looking at the personalities of screen-dependent children, we find that three features emerge across the board for all three dependent subtypes. These three features are *apathy, ignorance,* and *arrogance.* Simon's case provides an example of how these character features can play out in a child's life.

Simon's Case

by Cynthia

Simon was a self-identified gamer who fit the Charmer personality type and had the distinction of missing more assignments than any of my other students as he approached the end of his junior year in high school. To be exact, he was missing fifty-seven assignments in one semester spread over four courses. And he did not care. He assured me that he was "really good on tests" and didn't have to do the "irrelevant and useless homework." Simon had used his Charmer skills to convince his parents that it was the school's fault for not knowing how to "reach and teach" him. Also at this time, his parents had recruited an attorney to represent them to get the school district to pay for private schooling for Simon.

Simon's plan for turning things around sounded good at first glance, except that soon it became clear that his no-homework strategy was not working. He carried three Fs in core subjects and would have to add another year of high school to graduate at this rate of progress.

Simon brushed aside my suggestion that he needed to do homework and study every day. He countered by assuring me that as soon as he completed high school he would enter a local community college to pursue an associate degree in game design. Simon told me that he was happy because he had heard that college was easier than high school, and he could get out early in the day—so he could go home and game.

I disputed Simon's logic. Actually, college-level work is not easier, and there is as much, if not more, homework as in high school. The big difference is that college instructors do not monitor a student's progress. It is up to the student to succeed. The instructors are used to teaching adults who are motivated to complete coursework and financially responsible for their education. Simon, a boy taken care of by loving parents all his life, had no such motivation. And he knew that sooner or later his parents would forget his missing assignments, and things would go on as normal.

Simon had the self-advocacy skill set of the Charmer. He was not making waves. He was going along. Dealing with his issue with screen media use was like nailing jelly to the wall. You knew he was spending way too much time in his room with the lights turned down, but when you tried to get him to comply with ordinary schoolwork requirements, he had a million excuses and as many grand plans for turning things around.

Simon possessed three characteristics of children who self-identify as gamers: apathy, ignorance, and arrogance. These three features developed in his personality to protect access to his dependency by baffling, distracting, and frustrating caregivers. This character structure also protected Simon from the experience of shame relating to his media use and lack of success in his life.

First, there was *apathy* to the point of *moral indifference*. Simon really did not care about school, and he did not care if his parents put pressure on him to do homework. He simply did not care. He assured me that he did not feel guilty about missing assignments or getting poor grades. He did not do the homework. In fact, he did not give his parents or anyone else the moral authority to tell him what he should do or what is right and what is wrong. Simon was morally indifferent to the fact that he was making a mockery out of his parents' ardent hope that he would succeed in school.

The second character trait Simon shared with many other self-identified gamer children was *ignorance* to the point of being delusional. Despite the presence of a strong IQ, he was several grades behind in everything and was woefully lacking in basic knowledge, such as not knowing who fought in the American Revolution or when it occurred. He confused the American Revolution with the American Civil War and did not know when that had occurred, although he thought maybe it was in the late 1920s. He had an embarrassingly low-level understanding of arithmetic operations. And though he could read fluently, he had no idea of what he had just read. He had no comprehension.

Simon, as is true in the case of many screen-dependent children, was ignorant of his own ignorance. He actually thought he had a test-taking system that worked. His reliance on this myth in the face of reality looked a lot like a psychiatric delusional state. He was clearly spending too much time alone in the dark in his room.

As I think about Simon, an ancient proverb comes to mind:

> He who knows not and knows not that he knows not is a fool. Shun him.

> He who knows not and knows that he knows not is a child. Teach him.

> He who knows and knows not that he knows is asleep. Wake him.

> He who knows and knows that he knows is wise. Listen to him.

Simon expressed his ignorance with an *arrogance* that suggested clinical *grandiosity* (as is seen in bipolar disorder, narcissistic personality disorder, and several other disorders listed in the *DSM-5*). Listening to him, I was reminded of the vocal interpretation that actor Robert Downey chose when he played Sherlock Holmes. Simon's tone of voice was pedantic, his prosody or accent was odd, and his language overly precise. His arrogant demeanor along with his comments about the absurdity of school gave one the sense that he felt he was a superior human being—definitely superior to all the other kids who *had* to do homework to succeed.

One easy, effective, and immediate action parents can take

If it is true that abundant face-to-face social interaction unimpeded by even the presence of a **handheld device** is essential to the development of identity and personality of children, how do parents actually do something about the issue? We suggest in Chapters 10 and 11 that writing a screen control plan may be the option of choice for many families where an issue with screen dependence is most severe. Some families may not need to do this kind of complete revision of family culture. Initially, parents may choose to use less draconian screen controls to good effect.

One action that parents can take is to simply have times when their children are not allowed to have a cell phone in their pockets. Additionally parents could—with their phone service provider's assistance—configure their children's device to get calls only from them or other designated callers. Or they could teach their children how to listen and how to ask questions that draw others out. Attentive listening requires patience and insight. Children who are comfortable with their own company, who have a strong sense of personal identity, possess these two essential personality features.

Our observation of the children we serve in tutoring and psychotherapy confirms Turkle's assertion that children come to their senses quickly once they do not have reflexive and impulsive access to cell phones. She cites research done at device-free summer camps that demonstrates that after a very brief period of withdrawal, most children are able carry on truly lively, informed, and mutually empathetic conversations with each other.[97]

In order to make the changes needed to restore sanity to their children's recreational screen media and social media use, parents need to realize they have not only the *moral right* but also the *moral obligation* to take back control. Parents may agonize for years about what to do concerning the problem or how to convince, cajole, or bribe their children into being more moderate screen media users.

They do not know that the solution is directly in front of them—*they*, not their kids, are running the show and *they*, not their kids, are the only ones who can put a stop to the craziness and dysfunction caused by their children's intoxication with screen media.

Three characteristics of screen-healthy families

In the chapters that follow, you will learn how to keep the Gangsters, the Golems, and the Charmers out of your child's bedroom. But first, let's take a look at the families of children who *do not* become enamored with video games and other screen media. We observe that three conditions exist in screen-healthy families.

1. The family *does things together*, for example, getting together to clean the yard on Saturday or going for hikes or bike rides together.

2. Family members identify with certain values that govern the way they interact with each other. These values prize self-responsibility, honesty, and caring.

3. People talk *with* each other all the time. They interact *with* each other, not *at* each other.

It is no surprise that these same characteristics are described in literature about types of family cultures that help family members with bipolar disorder and other serious mental disorders. A type of therapy called family focused therapy (FFT) has been the subject of research and has shown that if a family culture contains these three dynamics, family members suffering from mental illness are much more likely to regain stability, healing, and control of their lives.[98]

The term *self-responsibility* may be viewed by some people as hopelessly old-fashioned language. It is common practice these days for teachers, therapists, and psychiatrists to turn up their noses at parenting practices considered conservative, such as requiring children to say "Yes, sir" or "No, ma'am" or creating family norms that define strict parental expectations and rules. Over time in modern psychology, there has been a shift toward the belief that decisions should be made by consensus, and children should be left to find their way without having to deal with too many family rules.

Now, after years of seeing how fragmented families have become and how this fragmentation has become the breeding ground for screen and online dependence and a whole host of psychiatric issues in children, we, the authors, have come to appreciate the wisdom of a more conservative parenting philosophy. If being strict and requiring compliance with rules builds self-responsibility, so be it. Sometimes strong children need strong boundaries.

Occasionally, children get to self-responsibility by themselves with no prodding from adults. In these cases, some emotional pain caused by screen dependence will motivate a child to change. A client example comes to mind: a bright fifteen-year-old boy who had a puzzling antagonism toward all his teachers at school. Most children have teachers they like and teachers they don't like, but this boy hated them all. As we explored his bitterness, it became evident that he felt that most of the teachers he knew at school did not really care about their jobs. They were just going through the motions and were deadly boring.

Suspecting that he was projecting something he did not want to say about himself, we asked him to talk from the "I" position with regard to his criticisms of his teachers beginning with the statement, "I am boring." We went on from there.

At one point his face lit up, and he said, "I just realized that most of last night I played a video game with three kids who live in different places in the world and I really don't know one real thing about any of them or even if they are kids! I didn't spend any time on my homework and feel bad about all the stuff I haven't turned in. All I did was bounce around in my fantasy room all night long! I accuse my teachers of wasting my time but now I see I am wasting *my own* time. I am disgusted with *myself*!"

The client's parents followed up a couple of weeks later and jokingly asked if there was Prozac in the drinking water in the office. Their son had made a complete turnaround, and for the first time in a long time the parents and their son were getting along.

Once vexed with screen dependence, a child is not condemned to the life of the Gangster, the Golem, or the Charmer. Time and time again, once a child is freed from screen dependence, these patterns of behavior fall away to reveal the strong, caring, vibrant person who has been there, out of sight, for the entire time.

CHAPTER 6

Rules for Schools: What You Can Do to Make Sure Your Child's School Is Part of the Solution

Public schools are not doing a good job of educating children with screen dependence. By and large, teachers are not lazy or unmotivated—only a tiny percentage of those in the field are, which is true of any profession. Rather, *the system* itself has devolved to a point where the educational potential of many children is not being realized, especially for those children who would really rather be on their screen media than studying and doing homework.

What is going on and what does this have to do with screen dependence?

If we are looking for a cause for this demise, we must first consider that teachers are only one group of participants in the process. School administrators, parents, and students themselves are also stakeholders. And there are "invisible" participants, including the people who fund the school system in the state legislature and those who create and provide educational materials and methods to the system. In order to better understand what is happening in this system, it is useful to look at the *motivation* of all of these stakeholders as they grapple with the issue of falling academic standards and results in the face of the challenge posed by students' overwhelming preference for screen media over schoolwork.

- School administrators have become lax in enforcement of behavior standards because they are afraid of parents' complaints or legal threats. And schools have become top-heavy with administrators and short on service-delivery staff such as teachers, counselors, and special education coordinators.

- Students are successfully ignoring the requirements that their parents and school are putting on them.

- Parents back up their failing children and attack the school system, usually a particular teacher, because they feel guilty that their child is not succeeding and want to do something, although they know not what to do.

- Policymakers and funders in the legislature are powerfully motivated to push any approach to education that is both less expensive and marketed to be the "latest and greatest" way to educate the greatest number of students. This fascination leads to the use of teaching methods that are frankly boring, such as the endless completion of student learning packets, teaching to the test, and acceptance of larger and larger numbers of children in any particular classroom.

The school may unwittingly make the situation worse with its lockstep and program-controlled approach to teaching. There is no allowance for the learning needs of individual students or encouragement of creativity in the delivery of educational services. Screen-dependent children who tend to be easily bored are now crushingly bored.

In this kind of situation, the best students, those who earn good grades, are the ones who *do not* have a screen media use problem. Period. Given all the conflicting agendas in the education system, the rule of the day is "survival of the fittest." A student has to be strong enough to graduate himself, if he has to, because he is not going to get much help from the adults.

Any student who is not *motivated to survive* for one reason or another will start losing ground. Learning will not occur. A child has to fight for learning in this situation. If the child is screen dependent, he has an onboard motivational issue from the starting gate. He is probably sleep deprived and brain exhausted when he goes to school. His memory and ability to retain learning are seriously impaired. He is in grave danger of flunking so many classes that he is scheduled for summer school, faces the need to repeat a grade entirely, or is in danger of dropping out.

Here are some of the deficits we observe in this group of students specifically, most of whom are boys. Upon entering ninth grade, these screen-dependent children

- cannot read fluently;

- have difficulty understanding the use of punctuation;

- do not pause at the ends of sentences when reading;

- have vocabularies that would be representative of a typical fifth grader;

- have difficulty spelling or writing short paragraphs;

- cannot write a letter or email—everything looks like a text message;

- do not know basic math facts, such as multiplication tables;

- cannot read analog time, therefore, do not accurately sense the passage of time;

- cannot type or use a keyboard efficiently and use a variation of "hunt and peck";

- do not know, or care to know, basic historical facts, such as why the United States had a revolution, why the Constitution is important, or how government works;

- do not read for pleasure.

A good place to begin understanding the impact of screen dependence at school is to pop into a typical ninth-grade classroom, for example, a large high school in the suburbs of Seattle. The classroom for our "virtual visit" is located in one of many schools that provide educational services to the sons and daughters of workers in the information technology industry around Seattle that includes Microsoft, Amazon, Google, and Nintendo USA. At the front of the class, a young female teacher is delivering instruction in algebra to a group of twenty-five children.

Four or five of her students sit with hoodies pulled up over their faces. It is difficult to see their eyes because they are set back and covered on the sides by their hoods. The scene is spooky, reminiscent of a gathering of monks in some dark church in the Middle Ages. Within the hoods, if you look hard enough, you can see blinking blue lights signifying the presence of Bluetooth earbuds. The students are listening to music, using social media, or texting their friends. They are not listening to anything that the teacher is saying. Several other children, not hooded themselves, also wear earbuds, transfixed by a podcast of a recent program featuring several prominent game designers who recently presented at a local gamers' conference.

The students sit motionless. No one raises a hand to answer the teacher's questions. She ignores their lack of participation and continues with her introduction to quadratic equations. When she first came to teach at this school last year, she was shown a school policy that required students to put away their handheld devices during class. Initially, she tried to get her students to comply with the policy, but when she invoked the rule, confiscating cell phones for a couple of children and sending them to the office, they returned shortly thereafter with the building principal's blessing of their behavior and scolding of hers. The children's parents had called and protested the policy of disallowing the use of handheld devices in class. Under their pressure, the principal gave in and eventually reprimanded the teacher for her inability to work with the parents of her students.

Most of her screen-dependent students are currently getting Cs and Ds in math. About half of these students are at risk of flunking the semester because many have missed homework assignments. Parents of these boys have protested that their teacher does not give corrected and/or graded homework material back or go over mistakes with them in class. And parents complain that homework requirements are rarely written on the whiteboard before the end of class.

Teachers at this school are not required to review turned-in work for mistakes or student understanding. They are required simply to check whether homework was or was not turned in. In some school districts, tests are not returned because of the high incidence of cheating. A number of the screen-dependent students in this math class also receive special education services that support their general education classes during the week. There are social skills groups, learning strategies classes, and study skills groups along with some individualized tutoring delivered at the school. Even with enrollment in these classes, most of the students are still dropping behind age-matched peers and are incapable of mastering age- and grade-appropriate subject matter. They simply are on their devices and not cognitively present for instruction.

Schools make the situation worse by assigning screen-dependent children to special education

Damage to a child's academic potential begins the day he begins chronic recreational screen media use. His baseline skill level will stay at that point and move very little as he progresses through each grade at school. Thus, it is typical to see an adolescent entering the ninth grade with less than fifth-grade baseline knowledge in all subject areas.

At some point, the child's parents may become aware of his pitifully regressed skill and knowledge base and seek to address the problem with an IEP. This plan enrolls him in the school's special education program and provides some specialized instruction along with a lessening of requirements for progression through the grades. The idea is that the child has a learning disability and should get accommodations for it, in terms of both the physical setting at school and the grading system.

If you recall from Chapter 3, being screen dependent would not ordinarily qualify a child for special education. Overuse of screen media at home and school is a choice, not a brain-based impairment. Unfortunately, many screen-dependent children with no neurologically based learning disability or psychiatric disorder are given an IEP because school districts and medical providers do not take screen dependence into account. When screen dependence is included in the next edition of the *DSM*, there will be more opportunity for accurate diagnosis. This is not presently the case.

What results from this mistaken assignment to special education is the use of scarce educational resources for children who would not otherwise fit criteria for inclusion. Not only does the error result in a waste of resources and misunderstanding of the real cause of the child's problem, but it also results in the screen-dependent child getting educational services that are useless. The law that mandates educational services for people with learning disabilities, called the Individuals with Disabilities Education Act (IDEA), stipulates that all children in the United States are entitled to a "free and appropriate education in the least restrictive environment."[99] Putting a screen-dependent child in the system is not appropriate and is typically overly restrictive.

Given the fact that special education is an inappropriate service model for screen-dependent children, some parents have taken legal action against school districts to force them to provide appropriate educational services. To get the school district to pay for these services, parents have to prove that an alternative placement in private school will enable their child to achieve academic, social, and emotional milestones. This often occurs because many private schools have a zero-tolerance policy for screen media at school. These schools are doing a much better job of controlling screen media use than public schools because they are at liberty to expel a child if he does not follow the school's policy with regard to recreational screen media.

School districts do not like to finance private school education for children with IEPs. Given the threat of having to make substantial outlays of resources for private school placement, it makes sense for school districts to be proactive and put in place, and keep in place, policies that call for zero–personal screen media use at school. It also makes sense to complete a careful review of the reasons why a child is given an IEP, taking into account the possibility that screen dependence is a root cause of his academic failure instead of a learning disability.

As suggested in Chapter 3, an in-depth review of the educational assessment and IQ test used to set up the IEP will contain telltale markers of screen dependence largely in what it *does not* contain. If screen dependence *is* the culprit, one would not see the deficits in short-term memory, perception, and mental-processing speed often seen in ADHD and learning disabilities. And one would note the presence of abysmal performance results in all academic areas along with the comment from evaluators that the child must be depressed because he appears to be very tired most of the time.[100]

Five things schools and parents can do to remediate the poor organizational abilities of screen-dependent children

The most profound impairment we see in our client research of screen-dependent children is the impact of compulsive screen media use on personal organization.[101] As a direct result of too much recreational screen media or social media use, children show impairments in their ability to remember assignments, plan tasks and activities, organize themselves to meet these task demands, and produce an output. Their mental focus is always on screen media, and doing well in school occupies a very low priority in their mind. So what can be done to refocus them and improve their personal organization? You and your child's school can upgrade the organizational ability of children with screen dependence by including these five simple practices in the day-to-day life of *all* students.

First, all students should use a written daily planner. Your child's building principal should start and end her day by promoting a daily planner as an essential tool. The daily planner is *not* a media device; it is something that must be written in, and a student should never go anywhere at school without it. Using a daily planner helps students to visually track their daily assignments, quizzes, tests, and the critically important—and mostly forgotten until the night before or early morning—study time. In fact, many students do not factor studying into the equation of getting good grades, and using a daily planner can begin to build good study habits.

To help the students we serve, we developed a template for a daily planner (see pages 126–127) that contains all the essential categories for organization of both academic and extracurricular activities. Encourage your student to use a daily planner as follows:

- Write the details of each assignment (page and problem numbers) while in class. Do not wait until lunch or after school.

- If there is no assignment for a particular class, write NH (no homework).

- Make a check mark on all completed assignments.

- If an assignment is not completed, rewrite it in the planner for the next day.

- Write and highlight tests, quizzes, and projects. This will help these items stand out.

- Write study times for all tests and quizzes. Daily studying helps reinforce information.

Second, all homework should be posted every day in the same place in the classroom. Time should be provided at the beginning of every class for students to write down assignments. Unfortunately, many teachers assume that all students will remember homework assigned verbally at the end of one class when students are bustling to get to their next class. Many children, especially those diagnosed with ADHD, have difficulty remembering spoken instructions and need a visual prompt to pause and write down the homework assignment. There are four steps required to complete any homework assignment:

1. Homework must be written down.

2. Homework must be taken home.

3. Homework must be completed.

4. Homework must leave the student's home and be returned to the teacher.

As we have noted, the screen-dependent child's mind is often not focusing on what is going on in class. Schoolwork is not as exciting to think about as a child's favorite screen media. Because the homework completion cycle can break down at any of these four steps, it is important to analyze what is going on with a particular child when there is a problem with homework. Children tend to have patterns of dysfunction in this regard. For example, one child may write down the assignment and actually do the homework but then forget to bring it back to school. Another child might chronically miss writing down the homework, so he never gets it done.

Third, good homework completion practices should be observed. The "A" students we work with demonstrate the following four homework habits:

- They do homework in a location at home that is free of distraction and typically is not their bedroom.

- They turn off cell phones and other media devices not being used for homework.

- They do their most difficult assignments first.

- After homework is completed, they place completed work in the same folder every day, which is then placed in the same spot for pickup in the morning on the way to school.

We observe that "A" students *do not* use recreational screen media often. If a child is screen dependent, it is an uphill battle to get him to put his heart and mind into homework and studying. This is why we believe that even before homework issues are tackled, screen media use at home needs to be addressed and resolved. We have observed that once this is done, there is quantum positive change in a child's attitude, and this change includes formation of more successful homework and study habits.

Fourth, students should not be allowed to use handheld devices for personal use at school unless there is a genuine emergency. This restriction would include cell phones, tablets, and wearable media devices, such as smartwatches and Google Glass. If students do bring a cell phone, parents need to have it programmed only to receive messages from them or designated others, and, importantly, so parents cannot text their children unless it is an emergency. Parents can contact their cell phone provider to learn how to block all but essential numbers on handheld devices used by their children. If a student does attempt to use a cell phone for recreational purposes, it needs to be taken away by staff, and the student must receive a consequence for violating the rule. In this situation, the principal must support her teachers in enforcement of the zero–recreational use policy.

Fifth, rules governing use of screen media devices should be posted in every classroom and consulted when infractions occur. No argument should be permitted regarding violation of the rule. Teachers need ask only one question when confronted with a violation of the school screen media policy: "What is the rule?" And administrators should make sure that parents sign off on the policy as part of orientation during the first week of school. One of the positive outcomes of a zero–screen media policy is that the number of students cheating on exams will be greatly reduced. If students are permitted to have devices, there will always be those who use their device to photograph exams or text others to help friends with tricky questions on tests.

PLANNER SKILLS

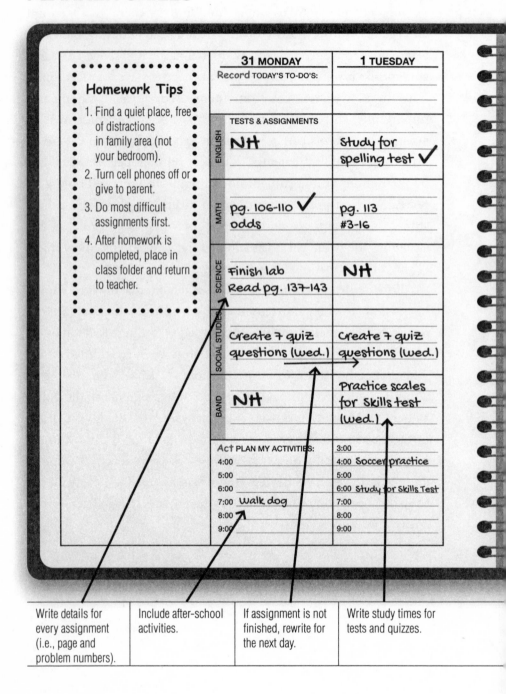

Homework Tips

1. Find a quiet place, free of distractions in family area (not your bedroom).
2. Turn cell phones off or give to parent.
3. Do most difficult assignments first.
4. After homework is completed, place in class folder and return to teacher.

	31 MONDAY	**1 TUESDAY**
	Record TODAY'S TO-DO'S:	
ENGLISH	TESTS & ASSIGNMENTS NH	Study for spelling test ✓
MATH	pg. 106-110 ✓ odds	pg. 113 #3-16
SCIENCE	Finish lab Read pg. 137-143	NH
SOCIAL STUDIES	Create 7 quiz questions (Wed.)	Create 7 quiz questions (Wed.)
BAND	NH	Practice scales for skills test (Wed.)

PLAN MY ACTIVITIES:

31 MONDAY	1 TUESDAY
Act	3:00
4:00	4:00 Soccer practice
5:00	5:00
6:00	6:00 Study for Skills Test
7:00 Walk dog	7:00
8:00	8:00
9:00	9:00

Write details for every assignment (i.e., page and problem numbers).

Include after-school activities.

If assignment is not finished, rewrite for the next day.

Write study times for tests and quizzes.

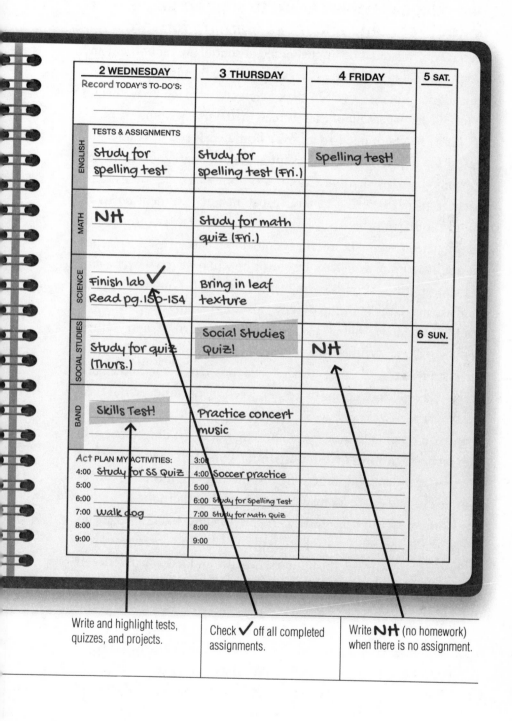

	2 WEDNESDAY	3 THURSDAY	4 FRIDAY	5 SAT.
	Record TODAY'S TO-DO'S:			
	TESTS & ASSIGNMENTS			
ENGLISH	Study for spelling test	Study for spelling test (Fri.)	Spelling test!	
MATH	NH	Study for math quiz (Fri.)		
SCIENCE	Finish lab ✔ Read pg. 150-154	Bring in leaf texture		
SOCIAL STUDIES	Study for quiz (Thurs.)	Social Studies Quiz!	NH	6 SUN.
BAND	Skills Test!	Practice concert music		

Act PLAN MY ACTIVITIES:	3:00		
4:00 Study for SS Quiz	4:00 Soccer practice		
5:00	5:00		
6:00	6:00 Study for Spelling Test		
7:00 Walk dog	7:00 Study for Math Quiz		
8:00	8:00		
9:00	9:00		

Write and highlight tests, quizzes, and projects.

Check ✔ off all completed assignments.

Write NH (no homework) when there is no assignment.

Two things schools can do to support screen controls at home and move learning forward

Screen controls must be implemented at school and at home if any progress is going to occur. Schools can do two things to support the educational process of screen-dependent students who have begun to receive management of their screen media use at home.

First, teachers need to go over homework the next day. The reason for homework is to prevent academic regression from the previous day's instruction. Completed homework can be used by teachers to evaluate the general capability of a student so as to sound the alarm if he is slipping between the cracks compared to age-matched peers in knowledge acquisition. Also, it gives a teacher the ability to know which topics she or he will have to go over again to make sure it sets in as permanent learning. If homework is not used as part of the learning process, it should not be assigned.

Unfortunately, many teachers do not correct and return homework, many times due to the socioeconomic conditions of their students. And some teachers do not check for homework every day and only check twice per week or on random days. At least once or twice per week, screen-dependent children take a chance on turning in homework, hoping not to get dinged because the teacher is simply not doing anything with the turned-in work. If screen-dependent children do turn something in, it is often a five-minute cut-and-paste job plagiarized from the Internet.

Homework can help students retain learning, but if teachers do not grade it and return it for students' review and correction, it is useless. This is why we, the authors, heartily endorse the practice of beginning each day with a return of homework and discussion of student understanding of the topic as revealed in their homework.

Second, schools should not allow IEP exceptions to requirements when screen media overuse is the culprit. Teachers often allow exceptions to requirements for homework if a child has an IEP. Typically this is because cognitive or emotional issues get in the way of knowledge retention or because a child is a slower mental processor, as is the case for most children with ADHD. We observe that many screen-dependent children push the limit of this benevolence; they simply refuse to do homework and let parents come up with plausible excuses. Allowing screen-dependent children to get away with not doing homework gives them the message that either parents don't really care whether they learn anything at school or they think their children are so dumb they could not do the work if they tried. Both messages are counterproductive to the learning process.

The best way to handle meltdowns at school

There are occasions when certain screen-dependent children and teens have a *meltdown* at school—a severe temper tantrum that may involve throwing things around, yelling, or threatening self-harm—when their screen media access is interrupted. This can be disruptive to the school community, as it is organized around the importance of order and routine.

Typically, school staff call the child's parents to come and get him. The child calms down immediately in his parents' presence. He goes home with them, and all is forgiven in the drama of the moment. They let him resume his screen media use at home so he can calm himself down.

Typically, violent behavior stops when school administrators, instead of trying to mollify the child or call his parents, call 9-1-1 or use school-based law enforcement staff to deal with the situation. Although the use of uniformed police officers to restrain a child may seem draconian, we observe that when this is done once, the situation rarely occurs a second time. This interrupts the reward cycle for the child who has learned that if he ups the ante with loud behavior, he will eventually get his way. With regard to having meltdowns in any situation, we borrow from ADHD wisdom—substituting the words *screen dependence* for *ADHD*: "Screen dependence is an explanation, not an excuse." There is no excuse for violent verbiage or behavior. Out-of-control students are simply not tolerated, and they are dealt with in a manner that anyone would be dealt with anywhere else in the community.

To bring about permanent change, parents and teachers need to work together

If schools adopt a zero–recreational screen media policy, screen-dependent students will howl loudly and fight back. Is it worth the fight? Let's review some of the potential benefits of following the suggestions contained in this chapter. Instituting screen controls at school in coordination with screen controls at home will

- bring some percentage of students who may be two to three grade levels behind their peers up to grade level;
- greatly reduce cheating and simplify administration of tests;
- result in homework completion and accomplishment of the purpose of homework in the educational process—to prevent academic regression;
- greatly enhance students' ability to pay attention and participate in class;
- markedly decrease the number of screen-dependent students who are erroneously assigned to special education services;
- improve the delivery of services to children who really need special education;
- reduce the risk to the school district of having to place children in private schools at public cost.

How a zero–recreational screen media policy at school contributes to identity development

In Chapter 4, we discussed how good conversational skills are essential for normal identity development in children.[102] We noted that it is through the give-and-take of conversation marked by attentive listening and limbic resonance that children gain the information and experience they need to nurture a strong sense of self and a strong and empathetic moral connection to others. Unfortunately, this important side product of being present at school is by and large sabotaged by the availability of cell phones, texting, and social media.

It is ironic, given the active damage that screen media have on social identity development, that many schools now have social skills programs as part of their daily curricula. These classes were originally developed to serve children on the autistic spectrum who were born with communication disabilities. Now they are widely used for *all* children, including many who carry no psychiatric diagnosis whatsoever.

From our observation, social skills curricula are not the answer for educators seeking to improve the ability of students to make friends and be successful socially. In fact, no resources need to be expended—the solution is right in front of educators. Schools would save money and help students achieve social and emotional milestones simply by forbidding the use of recreational screen media in the school building during the day. In the school's doing so, students would have to pull the ability out of themselves to communicate with each other.

Top Ten Excuses for Not Doing Homework

by Cynthia

Along with my yawn-o-meter for reading tired children, I have an alarm that rings in my head for homework excuses. As a parent, it might be handy to have this list at the ready. Here are the ten most popular excuses for not doing homework:

1. "I already did my homework."

2. "School is boring."

3. "Homework? I don't think I got any today."

4. "I'll do it tomorrow at school."

5. "I already know this; it shouldn't take me more than fifteen minutes."

6. "I'm waiting for a friend to text me the assignment."

7. "Homework is just busy work, and no one cares if I do it."

8. "I'm really good at test taking, and homework doesn't matter in this class."

9. "I am too overwhelmed. I am going to bed."

10. "The [insert class] teacher never tells us what the assignments are. Ask anyone."

CHAPTER 7

Give Me What I Want and Nobody Gets Guilt: How the Screen-Dependent Child Trains His Parents

Years ago we did a workshop at a local community college for parents of young adult learners with various learning disabilities who were enrolled in a degree-granting program at the college.[103] There were about twenty people in the room, parents of sons and daughters diagnosed with conditions including autism, dyslexia, executive function issues (severe disorganization), cognitive delays, and other serious learning issues.

At one point, after an hour or two of discussion, we asked participants whether they shared anything in common. Everyone in the room agreed that the one thing they all had in common was that they all felt *guilty* for the troubles their children had experienced. They felt a sense of guilt either for genetically giving their children the conditions that made their lives so difficult or because their children's difficulties in life were the result of bad parenting.

Why parents experience guilt and what it has to do with screen dependence

Guilt serves a function for human beings. It helps people feel a sense of *redemption* from the wrongs they believe they have inflicted on themselves and others. They punish themselves with it to get closure on the matter. Guilt can be thought of as an internalized parental voice that replaces some real authority figure. The voice of guilt may be quiet or shrill, and it becomes the self-punishment people generate to atone for their wrongdoings and thereby clear their minds and psyches of the memories of these transgressions.

Guilt manifests itself when people believe they have committed sins of commission and sins of omission. In other words, people do things they shouldn't, such as steal or lie, or they don't do things they should do, such as provide for their family. Modern parents carry a strong sense of both transgressions.

- "If I had paid more attention to her, she wouldn't have the problems she does now."

- "If we hadn't been such workaholics, he wouldn't have gotten depressed and angry."

- "If we hadn't been so heavy-handed, he wouldn't be so uncooperative now."

- "My child got his difficulties from my genetic line. I am surely to blame for the troubles he is having in life now."

- "She is lonely, and this breaks my heart. I have not done enough to bring friends into her life."

- "He is bored, and I have not done enough to help him discover things to be excited about."

The list goes on and on. Many parents do not spend one day of parenthood free of guilt. Parents' transgressions may be real or imaginary, but the struggle to survive financially in modern times, along with shifts in traditional family systems and values, gives parents many reasons to blame themselves. As stated previously, blaming yourself for being absent in your children's lives is a bum rap. Yes, parents are not present as much as their children need them to be, but they have not been playing; they have been *working* because they need to. Compared to the cost of living in the United States, salaries and benefits have been going down, not up, in the last thirty years. Today's parents forget that *their* parents and grandparents were hardly paragons of virtue when it came to being sufficiently present in their lives. There was the Great Depression, two world wars, the Korean War, and the Vietnam War.

The experience of parental guilt is understandable, but feeling guilty makes things worse when it becomes a weapon used by screen-dependent children to get their way. Likely it never occurs to the children that guilt-tripping parents could give them so much power, until their parents let them know how guilty they feel for all the things they believe they have done wrong.

In a real sense, guilt-tripping in this context is a *learned* manipulative strategy. If parents do not feel guilty or express verbally and nonverbally their sense of guilty regret for things, their children will not try to use it to control them. We notice that in the happiest, healthiest families we work with, parents model humility, self-acceptance, and disdain for useless guilt. It just gets in the way. It is not as though guilt-free families are sociopathic; they express the same level of caring as other families. But they do not spend a lot of time regretting personal action in the past or worrying about the future. The focus is instead on promulgating an ethic of self-responsibility and positive problem-solving.

When parents feel guilty about their performance as parents, their children pick up on that guilt and use it to sway the parents in a variety of subtle or overt manipulations. Children may

- become visibly depressed and anxious when screen play is limited by parents;

- show apathy even when presented with things they enjoy;

- voice loneliness and the belief that there is no joy in life, not even in friendships;

- accuse parents of always working and never being there for them;

- feign suicidal intent or make toss-off comments about killing themselves;

- avoid contact with other family members and ensconce themselves in their rooms; or

- appear helpless, tearful, and incapacitated in the face of requests to do homework or chores.

If a child plays the game of manipulating his parents effectively, he may gain freedom from

- responsibility to do anything but the absolute minimum of homework;

- criticism for his abysmal grades in the face of his strong IQ; he and his parents will unite in blaming the school and his teachers for not doing their jobs;

- responsibility to do any chores around the house, including cleaning up the old food materials scattered around his room;

- requirements to participate in the family in any meaningful way; when he does consent to being present at a family event, you know he is always waiting to get back to his screen pursuits; or

- any pressure to get a job; parents consider themselves lucky that at least he is not out doing drugs or getting into trouble, and they do not push him to work outside the home.

However the child comes to it, guilt will be the spearhead for his resistance to any attempts by parents to control his screen time. And generally it is a fine weapon for the job. Unfortunately, there are secondary impacts on his parents' relationship that the child does not understand. These secondary impacts include

- exhaustion of parents leading to a general lack of joy in their relationship. Nothing is fun anymore, including physical intimacy. A "chill" descends on the home;

- alienation of parents from each other, with each accusing the other of failing to manage their child's behavior. Mothers are often blamed by fathers for letting the screen-dependent child manipulate them, even though neither parent is in control of the situation;

- screen media overuse by one or both parents.

There is a stronger likelihood that *fathers* will have problems with screen media use, given that males of all ages are the biggest recreational screen media consumers. Our client wives often say their husbands come home, have something to eat, and then sit in front of their computers for the rest of the evening. Fathers often go into collusion with sons on this issue, and the home may develop a bitter feeling of resentment and defeat. At these times, the screen-dependent child may deploy the worst behavior, accusing his parents of fighting all the time and being negative—never realizing that *he* is the cause of their antagonism.

As the feeling of being a family crumbles, parents and the screen-dependent child learn that the most powerful force in their home is screen media. All tread lightly around it. No one tries to unplug media. No one dares to do so.

To regain control and purge the guilt, level with yourself, your spouse, and your children

Dr. Virginia Satir, the founder of the family therapy movement in the United States in the 1930s, suggested that attempts to communicate fail when people try to avoid accepting things about themselves that make them feel bad—things that are *guilt-producing*.[104] She observed that people tend to communicate through their mood and sense of self-worth. If they feel unworthy, broken, defective, out of control, or overwhelmed, they tend to use emotion-laden communication that goes nowhere and is subject to emotional manipulation using guilt.

In families, the flip side of guilt is heartless and cruel comments parents make to each other and the child in an attempt to regain control. Guilt is always accompanied by bitter resentment. Satir taught that people tend to use one of four predictable patterns of communication to avoid guilt and loss of control in communication. They blame others, try to placate others, become overly analytical, or they distract focus away from painful issues.

Satir said that *fear* is the force that pushes guilt, and once people can overcome their fear of making mistakes, making decisions, or expressing their feelings, they open themselves to a new way of communicating she called **leveling.** Satir was clear on the fact that people use leveling only if they feel good about themselves.

When you level with someone, you have the best chance of getting through to her or him and feeling good about your communication afterward. Leveling means you come to the other "on the level," as an equal, attempting neither to dominate nor give in to the other person. You approach with a certainty that you have something important to say or do and you do not let the other person distract you, threaten you, or guilt-trip you into giving up your position.

FOUR COMMUNICATION STRESS MODES

People avoid taking the risk of direct communication in predictable ways. These four forms of avoidance of "authentic" self-expression were codified by the late psychotherapist Virginia Satir. She said that individuals tend to favor a particular defensive strategy and that it is our fear, our particular "dragon," that drives our defensive communication style.

BLAMING

Personal Dragon
Fear of appearing weak and vulnerable. "I must always be right. I must always be strong. I must always be worthy. If I am not, it is your fault!"

Behavior and Feeling
In blaming mode, people insult, threaten, humiliate, or yell at others. One feels "hot," muscles tighten, breath is shallow, and the voice is shrill.

PLACATING

Personal Dragon
Fear of being hurt or abandoned. "I am weak. I survive by never displeasing anyone. I control with sweetness and 'yes saying.'"

Behavior and Feeling
In placating mode, people do anything to avoid conflict. They typically agree to things quickly or have weak resistance to any demand put on them. They may also adulate passivity, believing that "getting angry is the worst sin."

COMPUTING

Personal Dragon
Vulnerability to unknowing humiliation. "I have never understood emotions and have been hurt emotionally as a result. The only safety is in emotionless computation."

Behavior and Feeling
In computing mode, a person does not move physically very much at all and typically assumes a "lecturing" or "analytic" body position, with arms crossed, one hand on the chin holding up the head, "heavy with all the facts." The internal feeling is one of muscular rigidity. "Computers" tend to be experienced by others as boring people.

DISTRACTING

Personal Dragon
Being accused of something, being held responsible. "I am afraid of being found out and will hide who I am with sleight-of-hand and sleight-of-mind."

Behavior and Feeling
In distracting mode, a person flits from topic to topic quickly, changes subjects, or draws attention to irrelevant facts or events. The internal feeling is "spacey," anxious, and ungrounded. Distractors tend to make people feel uneasy, jittery, and frustrated without really knowing why.

LEVELING

There are some specific behaviors that contribute to good communication, a style that we call *leveling*. This is a style of communication that reduces confusion and promotes understanding. To level with someone:

1. **Use "I" Statements:** Take responsibility for your own feelings and opinions, without disowning them or "smoothing things over."

2. **Describe Behavior Specifically:** Describe the situation in terms of actions, or results expected, using clear, specific behavioral terms.

3. **State Your Preferences:** Use the words "I prefer…" to introduce a request for behavior change. This gets both people out of the "Do it my way or else!" trap.

4. **Restate:** Occasionally check your understanding by telling the other person in your own words what she/he has just said. Or you may ask the other person for a restatement of what you have said.

5. **Check for Perception:** Check out how your message is being received by encouraging the other person to talk about his/her feelings or reactions to the discussion.

6. **Share the Conversation Time:** Talk only half the time; don't over-talk and don't interrupt.

For parents, the antidote to a child's guilt-tripping is self-acceptance. Parents will not be susceptible to manipulation once they realize that although they have done their best, the problem crept up on them, and now it's time to do something else.

In Chapters 10 and 11, we propose that this *something else* has two phases. In the first phase, parents lead family members in a courageous, vigorous, and difficult redefinition of the family's basic values and how these values are expressed between family members. In the second phase, parents implement a measured and data-based screen control plan that is as restrictive as the situation demands.

Children's recreational screen media and social media overuse is an epidemic, but one that can be controlled and remediated as surely as have any of the other epidemics that have challenged our survival in history. Satir's leveling method is a great tool for strengthening parents' ability to deal with this epidemic within their homes—at the local level—where the work needs to be done.

Leveling with Carl

by George

Carl, a very skinny thirteen-year-old, has been heavily involved in screen media for two years. He plays *Minecraft* and several online **role-playing games.** He also sends hundreds of text messages each week and sometimes stays up most of the night texting or, on two occasions, sexting to friends, some of whom he does not know in person.

Carl does not like homework and basically blows off his parents' attempts to get him to do it. He is highly capable intellectually but is getting mediocre grades because he either does not do homework or is drowsy to the point of dropping off to sleep in his first two classes at school. In tutoring at home, Carl has deficiencies in understanding the basics in most subject areas. Although not diagnosed as ADHD, he shows inattention, distractibility, and inability to focus strongly as is seen in moderate to severe cases of the disorder. Unlike most children with ADHD, he does not show evidence of short-term memory issues. And he *can* focus if he puts his mind to it.

Carl comes home after school and sits down at his device and gets into his game. After dinner he resumes and tells his parents that he is going to be at it for only an hour or so and then will do his homework. Unfortunately, he rarely completes any homework assigned but finds time to play online until at least midnight.

His parents, Dan and Sandra, did not know what to do. Carl stopped having much to do with friends after getting heavily into recreational screen media and, as is the case with many screen-dependent children, has developed a pronounced **social anxiety disorder.** He feels lost and self-conscious around other children and "does not know what to say." His parents have not cracked down on his play because they feel that his online friends are the only friends he has. To make matters worse, when Carl becomes frustrated with homework he closes the door to his room and either sobs to himself or yells obscenities. These kinds of meltdowns may go on for hours, and his parents feel powerless to help him. Carl's parents voice enormous guilt for letting the situation go on as long as it has.

Naturally, most parents want to spare their children pain, so they do not force screen limits on them if their children react with psychological pain or an emotional display. Carl's parents were not an exception to this pattern. Like most parents, they tried to minimize the problem: "Oh, I don't know. We try to keep a handle on his screen media use. You could probably describe it as moderate, though he gives us problems if we try to limit it." Translated: "He plays online in excess of ten hours a day and all day Saturday and Sunday. If we get in his way at all, he has a meltdown that can go on for a long time and results in him punching holes in the wall."

Sandra reported that stress from Carl's issues had led to a lot of arguing between her and Dan, and they both were experiencing a growing dislike for their son. She described

Carl as manipulative and whiny with a tendency to be emotionally vicious, using hurtful and profane language meant to make Dan and her feel guilty when he did not get his way. Dan and Sandra wondered if Carl was suffering from bipolar disorder or if school was to blame. Surely it was the school's job to teach kids, and looking at Carl you would think no one at school cared whether he received an education or not.

The first thing I asked Dan and Sandra to do was to journal Carl's actual screen media use for a couple of weeks. I gave them a copy of the Screen Media Use Recording Form to use as a template. By the time they came in for their next session, they had done their homework and had documented the problem well. Carl's favorite device was his cell phone, and he used it for up to twelve hours a day. His results on the Screen Media Use Recording Form suggested that he had a moderate to severe screen dependence. His current grade point average is a solid D, an academic result way below his potential.

The year before our meeting, Carl's parents had talked with the special education coordinator at his school about setting up an IEP. She had denied the request, so they scheduled a meeting with a private psychologist to do an educational assessment to identify any learning disabilities that might be present and interfering with Carl's success at school. The assessment revealed no learning disabilities, and the practitioner suggested that Carl simply had a motivational issue that might be better addressed with psychotherapy.

They gave me Carl's history. I was especially interested in anything in their narrative that suggested the presence of an autism spectrum disorder, bipolar disorder, ADHD, learning disabilities, or any other psychiatric condition that might have a bearing on parenting Carl. When I make recommendations, I must take into account learning issues, perceptual style, executive function, and other psychological dynamics that might have an influence on a child's ability to deal with parents tightening control of his screen media use. In Carl's case, I didn't note any significant brain-based impediments in his ability to respond to his parents' strategies to improve the situation.

Although Carl's behavior mimicked what is seen in children with ADHD—he was very disorganized, forgot things, would get overwhelmed by homework, and was inattentive and highly distractible—these features were not present before middle school and were more than likely a result of the stress he was putting on his brain with chronic screen media use. Another factor that ruled out ADHD was the absence of any issue (short of that caused by sleep deprivation) with short-term memory. Memory issues are universally present in children with ADHD but did not show up in Carl's previous educational assessment.

Additionally, I didn't see any condition that could be improved with psychotherapy or pharmacology. Carl had to feel some emotional pain and have some willingness to change to tolerate the stress of therapy or deal with the side effects of medication. He did not voice any ownership of his own issues and, in fact, had resisted coming to my office to discuss his lack of progress at school. Ongoing therapy was ruled out.

I advised Dan and Sandra that they needed to get control of the problem, and this meant they had to be prepared to hear a lot of guilt-tripping and emotional blackmail from Carl. I advised them to begin the process of writing a screen control plan, starting with a series of family meetings to redefine the family's value system, and eventually writing the standards of behavior for family members to guide their interactions.

Dan and Sandra were eager to get started, so we scheduled a meeting with Carl that would occur within a couple of weeks. This would give them time to start the **family values clarification process.**

The day for us to meet with Carl arrived. I opened the meeting and asked Carl's parents to explain the decision they had made with regard to Carl's screen media use and the structures that they were putting in place to enforce their decision. There was marked tension in the air. Dan and Sandra were not looking forward to dealing with his resistance to their plan. But they summoned courage, and Sandra led with a full explanation of what they were going to do.

The plan called for cessation of screen media use after 9:00 p.m., including cell phones, and the homework computer was to be placed in a homework room under electronic monitoring by parents. The plan also included provision for adjusting the settings on the household Wi-Fi modem to power down at the appointed time. Carl's parents had a Wi-Fi modem for their own use. Their system was protected behind a locked door.

The plan allowed Carl one hour of recreational screen media use on Friday and Saturday evenings. Recreational screen media use was banned on school nights, and the ban would be strictly enforced. If Carl's grades did not improve, the plan called for abstinence from recreational screen media use for the rest of the school year. Additionally, Carl was not allowed to take his cell phone to school, and Dan and Sandra were going to set up a regular email check-in with his teachers to coordinate Carl's work in school and make sure he was attentive and not dozing off in class.

Carl was dumbfounded by what he heard. After his shock passed, he looked at each of his parents, eyes squinting. His breath became loud enough to hear. "No!" he then screamed. "You will not! You will not! That is my phone and my computer. You will not take these things away from me! I will not stand for this! This is the only relief I get from your constant fighting with each other! That is the reason I never have any friends over! And this is all I have. You will not take this away from me!"

No one said anything for a few moments; then Dan spoke. I was relieved to hear him modeling the leveling approach in his delivery and tone. I did not want to lose the opportunity they had by getting into a pointless argument. I wanted Carl to see his father's cool determination. I wanted a certain *gravitas* in this moment. I wanted Carl to know, perhaps for the first time in a long time, that his dad meant business and would not back down.

"Carl," Dan began, "we've talked about your screen media overuse many times but have always let you have your way. Now we have to take a stand on this, Son. We are seeing you work way below your potential at school, fail in your social relationships, and lose any ambition to make something of yourself in life. We know you are a smart kid and could do better. Your mother and I are standing together on this. You will not turn us against each other or turn our intention around on this again. As night follows day, all screen media in our home, except family television, will cease at 9:00 p.m."

Carl began to cry. He pleaded for another chance. He promised to do anything they wanted to keep his current screen access. But his parents were resolute. After a few moments, Carl stopped crying, sat up, and looked at his mother fiercely. "Sandra," he began—using a parent's first name is a singular gesture of disrespect we have noticed among screen-dependent children—"how could you let him [referring to his father] do this to me? Don't you care about me? Or don't you care about anything but work, Mom? Right. Why do you think I became a gamer, Mom? Because you work all the time. Okay. So get over it. At least have the decency to give me another chance!"

Sandra also used the leveling approach in responding to Carl's plaintive attempts to make her feel guilty. "Carl," she began, "you never used this kind of language before you started gaming. It's done something to you I don't like. Your words do hurt me, but I'll get over that. The most important thing is that you come to remember that you are part of this family and only part of it. We are finally putting a stop to something that has gone on far too long. We can't tolerate what your gaming is doing to your mood or school success. We are putting a stop to it because we have to for you, and for us."

Carl continued to grumble and interrupt his parents as the meeting wound down, but for the first time he was hearing straight talk from his mom and dad about what they were really feeling. He did not say anything toward the end of the meeting and seemed to be resigned to the plan.

I could tell he knew in his heart they were right. Part of him was lonely for something he used to have with them. Even though his nervous system was still jangling from the news that he was about to go cold turkey, I sensed that he was getting a bit of insight into himself and taking some ownership of the situation.

Carl followed up with me after this session, and we committed to a plan for several more sessions in which we brainstormed and eventually implemented what his life would look like post–gamer phase. He was surprised to learn that the initial period of boredom after his evening play was curtailed didn't last too long. He had more time in the afternoon now. He linked up with some friends who loved tennis and was beginning to make his mark as a capable player.

And Carl decided to explore new-generation board games, bringing home one called Suburbia that had been lent to him by a neighbor. Newer board games, unlike board games his parents played such as Monopoly, require more than chance from the throw of dice to win. Players win by using thoughtful decision-making. Suburbia, unlike a video game, was interactive and social, and challenged players' critical-thinking abilities.

Toward the end of our work together, Carl confided that the reason he could stay the course and not fight his parents on the restrictions they put on him was because he felt so much better physically and mentally. He had energy. His grades had leapt forward from Ds to Bs in every subject. He was not depressed all the time. Girls were paying more attention to him. His social confidence was coming back.

Carl was enjoying secondary benefits of getting better control of his screen media use.

His dad followed up with me around the last time I spoke with Carl. Dan told me that his wife had said something to him that had given him the ability to drop the guilt he had regarding Carl's screen dependence. Sandra had told him to remember that all the craziness surrounding screen media is in "the air we breathe." She impressed upon him that no one is to blame here. And Carl had gotten the message, too.

The importance of parental self-compassion

In Carl's story, Dan and Sandra were on solid ground by first making the issue of screen control be about their ability to be *kind to themselves* instead of blaming themselves for Carl's continuing misfortunes. They also did not let the situation devolve into an argument that is either soon forgotten or goes on forever and results in nothing. They simply did what needed to be done and used the leveling style to keep on message and keep communications open and clear. Carl's parents began the process where it must start: by having the self-compassion to accept they had made some mistakes and now was the time to correct the situation. No one is perfect.

We all do the best we can given the information we have at the time. Parents forgive themselves once they understand that this problem has crept up on them slowly, over several years. It took a long time for parents to become so totally entranced by screen media that the media came to control them, and they did not even know there was a problem. Now there is research stating that it *is* a problem. The old bromide applies: "Fool me once, shame on you. Fool me twice, shame on me!"

Take heart, fellow parents! You can bring your son or daughter back to her or his senses. Literally. As in the case of Carl, you can return your progeny to her or his natural state of well-being. Once you are a few weeks into the process, you can relax a bit. If you are like most of the parents we have worked with who have taken on this challenge, you will be handsomely rewarded when your child's personality comes back. Your child is in there, and although you might have to fight through the underbrush to pull him out, he is worth the fight.

CHAPTER 8

Boys Against Moms: The Hidden Anguish of Mothers and Wives

Although the reasons are unclear, boys and men form the deepest attachments to screen media involving gaming and experience the deepest states of screen dependence with that form. Girls are much more likely to develop social media dependence and less likely to compulsively play video games.[105] Let's take a look at how these patterns begin and how they express gender-role differences in American culture.

In the modern household, it is difficult to differentiate constructive from destructive media use because both parents frequently have to be on their devices after they come home, well into the evening. Women are less likely to have a serious problem with evening online use and more often hit the power-down switch when the work is done and turn to their family for contact and sharing. Female clients regularly report that when they get off the computer, they find themselves looking at the backs of the heads of their husbands and children who are hunched over their devices, lost in the online trance.

Invisibility of women regarding this issue, and many others, is related to societal norms that consider their lives less important than the lives of men. In 96 percent of American households, women are the lead parent, and they have both career and homemaking duties while their husbands only have to focus on their career. Even though both parents may work full-time, when dad comes home, dinner is ready for him, and there is no expectation that he hassle with the children's homework or bad screen habits. In only 4 percent of households do fathers play the lead role of being both breadwinner and homemaker/homework monitor.[106]

A third of households in the United States are run by single parents, with a higher percentage of custodial parents being women.[107] We have observed that if custody is shared, then the most screen media use typically occurs at the father's residence. If a mother has stronger boundaries around screen media use, she will get the full brunt of the child's anger upon his return from visiting his dad. We have also observed that if the mother is able to deal with her child's anger and pestering, she will be able to maintain control. Things usually settle down in a day or so. The fact that this happens at all is a testament to the power of screen media to induce psychological states in children that have side effects—chronic play at Dad's house causes mood dysphoria at Mom's house.

In a single, blended, or traditional family setting, the mother-child relationship is primary, so mothers tend to be highly attuned to the nervous systems of their children and the first to note a disturbance in a child's developmental pattern. And wives tend to be the ones who first notice the demise in quality of their contact with their husband based on screen media overuse. Wives are the first to feel the loneliness of invisibility and are often the ones who initially demand that changes be made.

But once again, the realities of modern life come to the forefront. Screen media are an extremely inexpensive baby sitter, and the boss wants both parents thinking about or working at the job at all times during the week. If she demanded that her husband actually come home emotionally and psychologically at 5:00 p.m., his career advancement might be jeopardized. Typically fathers are pleasant, but not present, in the evening.

Changing the status quo is about reducing forces that resist change and building forces that drive change. In this situation, economic necessity has a booming voice—it is the most powerful force resisting change in screen media use toward nondependence as opposed to chronic dependence. At some point, however, as the emotional pain connected with a screen dependency in the family begins to exceed the fear of changing the economic status quo, parents may elect to assume more control over their children's screen media use.

Typically, it is the wife who starts talking about reducing the time her husband spends online in the evening and limiting the time her children spend online, seven days a week. Also, typically her husband will give her lip service for the need for change, but he does very little to enforce new rules around screen media use. His voice is absent in this conflict. Mom does all the enforcement because typically Dad makes more money in his job and doesn't have the time to deal with it.

As parents, either separately or together, begin limiting access to screen media, their child may use his father's screen media use as his strongest argument for them to back off. "How can you tell me I have to be off everything by 9 p.m. when Dad is online until 1 a.m.? It's not fair!" This argument pits the husband against his wife by making him defend his own screen practice as nonchronic even though he may have an issue with overuse himself.

Or a father may actually bond with his son or daughter by using screen media *with* him or her. It is never easy to gain a child's confidence, but now the father notices that if he lets the child have free access to screen media, he is much more interactive and relational with him. The child's delight in talking about his game extends even to his father, who is in turn pleased to finally get his son's attention. Now enter the possibility that the father has always enjoyed spending a lot of time with his computer, and the two of them have powerful forces resisting any change in the status quo.

Once a father joins with his son or daughter in screen play, an inevitable conflict may arise between the mother and all other family members. She now becomes the official spoiler. When this happens, the parents go into conflict with each other, which may take several forms. The father may simply not support her requirements for more moderate screen media use. Or he may be more covert in his resistance, undermining her by always having excuses for his own screen media overuse and being lax in enforcement of household screen media rules.

Sons listen to their fathers' voices differently than they do to their mothers' voices. Typically they pay attention to the male voice. They either obey their father or overtly resist his rules. They often accuse their mother of yelling at them even when she is speaking in a normal tone of voice at normal volume. The process of listening is an emotional process as well as a mechanical process, and it is the boy's need to emotionally separate from his mother that results in the amplification of her voice in his ears.

Power strategies used by screen-dependent daughters when parents get into this crunch typically involve *passive resistance*. Generally, the daughter will humor both parents equally. Enforcement of any new screen media use rule is usually left up to the mother. If her mother has the gall to press the point and require the daughter to get out of bed and go to school, she resists moving and speaks to her mom with contempt. She knows her father will not physically support moving her, and eventually her mother will give up. The daughter may then stay in bed with her cell phone, possibly hiding behind a psychiatric diagnosis of depression.

This is a formula for endless conflict in the family, and the damage can go deep and wide. Whether it is parent-against-parent or child-against-parents, mothers and fathers come to the sad conclusion that they don't like a particular child. This conflict further impairs the child's developmental process because emotional attachment is needed if the child's cognitive and emotional capabilities are to mature. If the status quo is going to change, fathers need to get into the fray.

Where have all the fathers gone?

Fathers are more drawn to screen media themselves, less biased against its use, and more apt to deny that it is an issue with their children. They are more apt to let it happen because of their experience and enculturation. The fact is that by and large, fathers are *absent* when it comes to controlling household screen media use. Absence of fathers in controlling children's screen media use must be seen in the larger context of the absence of fathers generally in the day-to-day lives of their families in the twenty-first century.

Societal norms boost the importance of male wage earners and reduce the status of female workers as well as furthering gender-based wage inequalities. Women are invisible, and men benefit from this invisibility. Women have to do two jobs, not just one. They are expected to work outside the home as well as be the primary homemaker after work. And they earn, on the average, less than 79 percent of what men earn in the United States for the same work.[108]

Other norms stipulate that a man's basic importance equates to his monetary worth and ability to make money, while a woman's importance equates to her social and emotional skill level and her ability to make people around her feel good. These values get men off the hook for management of family issues, and yet they continue to control the lives of millions of women. Although mothers and wives may attempt to control screen media use at home, they lack the power to do so without participation of their husbands who are often not around.

Poor relationships that men today had with their own parents, especially their own fathers, are an important contributing factor for the absence of the father. Fathers learn how to parent from their own fathers. By example and action, a man is well equipped as a parent if his own dad showed him how to deal with his own emotional issues. This gives him the skill to help his children with their emotional lives. Strong fathers have a good understanding of when to hold firm boundaries and when to let things go. Unfortunately, many of today's fathers did not experience a loving relationship with their own dads and have no example for nurturing emotional connections with their children. Many modern fathers lack insight and foresight in their own emotional lives, and they lack the courage to admit feelings of shame and vulnerability around their roles as fathers. So they walk away and leave their wives to deal with the situation.[109]

Part of the issue also stems from the poor relationships that men have with each other. Unlike their wives, many husbands do not have guy friends. Men are acculturated to go it alone. In fact, after years of emotional isolation, many men *do not* want friendships with other men or anything that takes time away from work. This lack of peer bonding deprives fathers of valuable information they could be getting from each other about parenting. Most important, it prevents them from experiencing the mechanics of building rapport with other people in their lives at a deep level. Isolation from friends makes it hard for men to know how to have a conversation with their children. They do not understand the value of walking, talking, and hanging around with their sons and daughters. Learning how to be a friend with another man helps them be better husbands and fathers.[110]

Fathers must be equal partners in the process of screen media management if there is going to be any change in the status quo.

This process begins with awareness of the fact that they are indeed largely absent from the fray and must become much more involved if there is going to be a change for the better.

A note of hope

Our client experience informs us that children and young adults can overcome screen dependence and get their lives on track. All children are capable of rewriting their own great story, and sometimes the special voice of a father is needed to get the program on track. It is never too late to help a child get back into the world he was born to enjoy. Financial guru Suze Orman puts it succinctly: "People first, then money, then things."[111]

For fathers, putting people first, in this case themselves and their families, may require that they take the risk of pushing for a regular nine-to-five work schedule so they can spend some quality time with the people they love and who love them. For fathers who accept the challenge, getting better control of a screen media use problem can be a breakthrough life experience.

The reason many fathers become absent to the issue is that they have been brainwashed to believe that they do not deserve to take better care of themselves. They are taught to believe that work always comes first, and when not working, they should be thinking about work. To misquote the captain in the movie *Cool Hand Luke,* "What we have here is a failure to *imagine!*"[112] Fathers *can* wake up from the trance their upbringing has put them in and really start enjoying the presence of their children, even fighting for it by wearing the symbolic black hat when it comes to managing a particular child away from screen dependence.

Steve's story of coming home

Steve, a man in his early fifties, came in for counseling with his wife Rena to discuss his own distress in managing the video game compulsion of his twelve-year-old son, Ethan. Steve explained how his resolve to better control his son's screen media use had changed his life. And, as is frequently the case when people change their beliefs and perspectives, Steve changed his attitude toward gaming as the result of a near-traumatic incident.

Steve recounted that he had never had a problem with Ethan's gaming. He said that his son had a bad temper, and it had gotten him into trouble at school. He also did not have many friends. So for a couple of years, Steve and Rena allowed Ethan to have free rein to access screen media. They gave him an Internet-capable cell phone and wide latitude with most of his screen media.

Problems at school in both academic and social domains had alerted Ethan's parents that he was not getting anywhere near enough sleep. He had also developed a hair-trigger temper that would go off whenever he did not get his way, usually including "f-bombing" one or both of his parents.

Several weeks before he came to counseling, Steve had attempted to put ordinary limits on his son's gaming—on that particular day he described how the boy had been playing *Grand Theft Auto 5* for about five hours, stayed home sick from school, and was in a foul mood. When Steve told his son he was putting limits on his game play, Ethan became enraged and threw his laptop computer out of his bedroom window, almost hitting a passerby on the sidewalk outside their apartment. Police were called.

Rena could not stop crying after the police left. Steve comforted her and realized that he was letting her down by keeping himself out of the issue of Ethan's screen media use. This event scared Steve into becoming more involved in managing Ethan's screen media time.

Before their first session, they had done their own data gathering and assessment using the BIGS-P and Screen Media Use Recording Form. In the meeting, we worked on putting together routines for Ethan that would help him get out of his room and into real life. Although he was still resisting limits, his parents had resolved to limit their son's recreational screen media use. They had worked out a schedule to look at the values that defined them as a family and wrote a set of behavior standards for everyone in the family, including themselves.

Steve and Rena had decided not to use a formal level system but instead were holding onto the possibility of using one as Plan B. Importantly, Steve was now fully involved and working with Rena to bring things back into balance with screen media use in their home.

Steve felt a new energy in getting more control at home. He related that he was also getting back into golf, a game that he loved for the exercise, fun, and opportunity to be alone. He went on to say that he was "giving golf back to himself," and he now knew that in taking back his place in his family, he was reclaiming his own life.

Rena sat by his side, her eyes welling with tears. "I feel like Steve's come home and I feel like I will get back my son." She paused and made intense eye contact with her husband for a moment. In this moment Steve was making an unspoken promise in that shared gaze: She was right. She was getting her son *and* her husband back. She could count on it. Their life as a family would be whole again.

To: Fathers and husbands
From: George
Subject: Common life patterns for screen-dependent sons as they grow from boys to men

Got a minute?

I am a father of three adult children. I am proud of all of them. They live with heart and purpose, and I wish the same for your sons and daughters! I am also a mental health counselor who on some days feels like a walk-on for the movie *Invasion of the Body Snatchers*. So many of the children I work with in my practice come in pitifully disabled by screen media overuse; they are not mentally present with me. The research is clear that chronic screen media use causes children to get depressed, anxious, agoraphobic, apathetic, and socially isolated. On top of all those impacts, it makes boys into physical weaklings. And it's pretty clear what the solution is: No more than an hour per day of gaming, YouTube, or social media without interruption for moving around and exercising out the carpel tunnel. No weekend binges. Period. Even better, no recreational screen media during the week.

Students who receive "A" grades do not play video games or use a great deal of recreational screen media. Period.

Of course, you may say, that all may be true, but I have to work—and my wife too—and it's a great babysitter and may actually benefit my child in different ways.

Contrary to the myths propagated by the screen media industry, screen media use *does not* build character. It teaches kids how to play the game according to the game writer's rules and strategies. Video games do not improve reaction time. They do not build imagination. They will not make him a better driver or a more creative person. If he is good at the game, he is simply good at playing by the rules set by the game manufacturer.

I would have to agree: screens are incredibly efficient babysitters. But let me also suggest that there is a price to pay for the free time you get. Here is the pattern that your son may exhibit if he is like many of the children and young adults I have worked with in my psychotherapy practice.

Sometimes seeing the whole pattern is useful when one is deciding how to deal with an issue.

THE PATTERN

If your son has been involved with recreational screen media, particularly gaming, for more than an hour each day since grade school, by ninth or tenth grade you will see slippage at school. Any subject that is difficult for him will become nearly impossible. And you will be tormented by the feeling that you should do something to help him, but you will not know what that help should be.

Some percentage of children in public school drop out before graduation, and these children begin showing patterns associated with dropping out by the fourth grade.[113] One warning sign is that a particular child begins missing school frequently. Children similar to your son, who spend a lot of time home sick and on their screen media, would be included in this population. After a while there does not seem to be any point in going to school at all. Nothing is as interesting to the child as his screen media. Ask him. He will tell you exactly that.

You probably want him to be good at critical thinking, even creative thinking. You want him to be able to plan things out a bit and have some ambition for his life. If he continues his screen media overuse practice, by the time he is sixteen years old or so you will notice that he has little critical-thinking skill or interest in his future. In addition, his understanding of aspects of modern life that you take for granted will be woefully lacking. He will not know basic facts about current or historical events, such as when World War I or World War II started. He will know nothing about the Vietnam War, the Iraq War, or the events that led to these wars. He will not read for pleasure. He will not know his multiplication tables. He will not know or understand the details of writing an essay. His written production of an essay or email will look like a variation of a text message.

And it will be very difficult for him to *imagine* his own future, what he wants to do, and where he'd like to do it. He will be quite impulsive. Because of issues at school and because he will not be interacting much with his mother or you, you will become concerned and take him to a psychiatrist for medical evaluation. Your doctor will diagnose him with an anxiety disorder and depression and probably will not say anything about screen media overuse because he will not be knowledgeable about its impact. Or the doctor may diagnose him with mild ADHD and assure you that once you get your son on medication everything will be okay. Medication may help a little, but it will become clear that it does not help your son much with his struggles at school and home, and he will stop taking the medication.

Your son's screen dependence will change his personality. Surprisingly, you will discover that he does not care to go through the hassle of getting a driver's license. He will not really be into cars. He may not have friends of the opposite gender. Most of the gamer kids he talks to will be boys whose age will span middle school to young adult. You will notice that friends do not come around, and if they do, they all immediately go to his room to game.

He and his gamer friends will also act sexually immature and feel anxiety in their relationships with girls. If your son is similar to 80 percent of boys who spend a majority of their time online, he will have accessed a lot of porn by the time you discover it on his computer. Unfortunately, this practice will give him a skewed idea of male-female relationships. Porn teaches all the wrong lessons to boys about forming relationships. It erodes the boy's respect for himself and women.

He will have poor social confidence and will become withdrawn and look troubled. He will avoid novelty, especially social novelty. And he will use a variety of manipulative ploys to protect his access to his screen media use.

By his mid-teen years, you will become uncomfortable with the way he *looks*. His chest will be flat, and his body will look soft. He will appear weak, with no muscle definition. He will have the pallor people get when they spend too much time in darkness, and you may find yourself wondering if he has a vitamin D deficiency.

Later on in his teens, to appease his mom and you as well as to continue to get your financial support, he will get a menial part-time job that does not challenge Internet or gaming time. Or he will not get out of the house at all after high school and will remain unemployed. He will stay in his room on his devices into the early morning hours and will sleep in until eleven o'clock or later every day.

If he graduates from high school, he will do so with grades that do not show his potential. He may, however, have no problem being accepted by a public university. Now that public, four-year colleges and universities cost upward of $28,000 each year, they are more likely to accept anyone who can pay the tuition. He will assure you he can make it through successfully, although his specific career plans will be unclear. He may initially elect to take an academic major that he cannot handle intellectually, which shows the grandiosity that comes with being a master-level video game player for years. That may be good as far as that goes, but it actually goes nowhere in terms of helping him in the real world.

If he is like a third of students now entering college, he will have to take several remedial writing and math courses before he can get into his program in earnest. Remember, the meter is ticking at $28,000 per year. By the middle of his sophomore year, if he makes it this far, his screen dependence will take him down, and he will drop out. This will be the logical consequence of electing to play instead of study. He may try to fake it for a term or two, taking your money and not going to class. But eventually college will stop, and he will come home.

He will return to the safety of his room until he is twenty-eight, twenty-nine, or thirty-two. At some point he may get into a relationship and will start putting pressure on you to let her move in or to pay for an apartment for the two of them as they contemplate getting married. Getting married may sound good to you. Normalcy at last. But please understand he has not learned how to be independent.

He will spend your money experimenting with a variety of occupations. First, he will try his hand at expensive specialized technical schools that serve the gaming industry and will drop out when it gets too difficult. He will discover that there are very few good jobs in the gaming industry. In fact, when anything gets too difficult, he will reflexively drop out. He may get other inspirations, but as his sedentary lifestyle settles in, he will begin to feel like he is a disabled person—disabled, of course, by his high anxiety and chronic, low-grade depression. By his mid-twenties he may complicate the picture with overuse of pot or booze, or both, as he sits down to play, and he will start putting on weight.

THE END RESULT

You will not enjoy your life as his caretaker, and the stress of his presence will put pressure on your marriage. You and your wife will stop having fun together. The color will go out of your relationship as you deal with the relentless low-level stress of your adult child's depression, apathy, and agoraphobia.

By the time you and he walk into your psychiatrist's office to get him certified as permanently disabled—so that he can apply for **Supplemental Security Income (SSI)**—you both will have lost any of the pride that, up until that point, kept you from having him certified as incapable of taking care of himself.

I do not, of course, know your child's situation, or your personal situation. I write this from the perspective of an observer and reporter of the experience of families I have worked with in my counseling practice.

The good news is, if you get on this issue early, your son may turn out just fine. Research indicates that early intervention is the best way to go. His life can be saved, but it will take some work on your part, on his mom's part, and on his part, too.

Thank you for taking the time to read this letter.

CHAPTER 9

Surrender Is Easier when You Have Good Reasons: What Parents Tell Themselves to Stifle the Inner Voice of Concern

There is no doubt that the world is experiencing the Golden Age of Electronics as formative on civilization as the Bronze Age or the Renaissance. The growth of technology sparkles like a night in Las Vegas.

Humans share the air they breathe with billions of invisible electronic connections. The digital information revolution, which began with the development of the integrated circuit and the birth of the Internet, has grown into its adolescence. Still largely unregulated in the free world, the Web grows in leaps and bounds daily, with more intelligent technology surrounding everyone like a purposeful cocoon.

The Web's lifeblood is information, and its purposes are generally to get people to buy something or believe something. The technology that drives it is machine and application based and has the spirit of a geometric progression: each new successful application creates new potential and opportunity for many more like it.

People buy something by touching their cell phone to someone else's cell phone. Their cars warn of impending accidents, compute and execute evasive action, and even drive by themselves. People talk to their cell phones, and they talk back, providing instantaneous data on anything happening in the world at that particular moment.

As the revolution proceeds, the growth of virtual worlds takes place on the Web with screen media such as *Second Life*. Not too far from the holodeck featured on *Star Trek,* which is set in the twenty-sixth century, a person using *Second Life* can choose an avatar that represents her- or himself and have a complete, albeit virtual, life.[114]

Then there is gaming technology, which is amazing, electrifying, and entrancing. It is easy to see how a lonely child with few real friends could get lost in that sparkling world and come to identify himself as one of its denizens. If he cannot have friends in his neighborhood, he can be Lord Master of some domain that spans continents and includes thousands of other children who would love to be Lord Master.

Twenty years ago, a child had to tough it out at school. He would either learn how to make friends or would grow up a loner. He would learn, outside his home, how to fake it and/or make it through school. As a young adult he would hope to find a particular interest that had enough charm to pull him permanently into its service—a vocation—or he would be lost and drift without really knowing his role. As he matured he would have to use his imagination to survive, and by age eighteen he would be expected to know that he needed a plan to make it on his own.

That scenario has changed by virtue of the intersection of two forces in modern life: the growth of the Internet and the growth of corporate power. On one hand, the growth of the Internet has provided a virtual substitute for the tasks required to meet the *core developmental needs* of the child and adolescent—to experience independence from his parents and feel autonomous and capable in the world. The teenager no longer has to work some menial job to give himself a sense of worth and productivity. He now tests himself with sleep deprivation, making mock war on a virtual enemy online. The Internet has given him rites of passage that may damage his brain over the long run but don't hurt his body in the moment.

More importantly, technology has given his parents a babysitter. Beginning with the demise of the unions in the United States in the 1960s, corporations have assumed more authority in the lives of people. They work to maximize profit and in so doing have eliminated generous salary structures for all but the highest-level administrators, essentially forcing both parents to work to make ends meet.

A mother now works a nine-to-five job, and a father usually comes home an hour or so later than she does every night. They may still be on their computers serving their corporate masters until 7:00 p.m. or 8:00 p.m., and they do not want to be interrupted. They cannot be interrupted. Dinner is perfunctory. Quick. Check in on homework. Eat food. Get back to the computer or cell phone.

If parents can afford it, they load after-school activities on their children so that they are doing something away from their screen devices or because that is what families of a particular status are supposed to do. As mythologist Michael Meade puts it, modern life is about "measurements and appearances."[115] Parents work hard to upgrade their rank, status, and wealth. They cannot have their children getting in the way of this goal with messy developmental tasks. Although many parents report that they sense their screen-dependent children are missing something in terms of their social and emotional development, these parents are more terrified that the oppositionality and impulsivity—which emerge in all children during adolescence—will disrupt *their* lives. This fear of adolescent development is seen as subtext in all the reasons that parents give for *not* limiting their children's screen media use.

- "Without his online friends, he would not have any friends. Thank God for social media!"

- "At least he's not out getting drunk or smoking pot."

- "At least with the new game he is playing, he is getting outside and moving around."

- "At least he's not out getting into trouble like I did when I was a kid."

- "Actually, his gaming has improved his dexterity, coordination, and reaction time."

- "Actually, his gaming has increased his problem-solving skills."

- "Actually, his gaming has developed his imagination and creativity."

- "Actually, his gaming has developed his critical-thinking ability."

- "If we send him outside to play, he will be alone. There are no kids at the playground."

- "We can't do anything about it anyway; he'll just go to his friends' homes and game there."

- "We are proud of him. When he finishes high school we're sending him to DigiPen for a college degree in writing games. Looks like he has found his passion!"

- "Actually, school is to blame. The educators have not been able to reach him, so how can they teach him?"

And there is psychological pressure that pushes denial. Most parents do not want to be seen as bad guys in the eyes of their children who were really cooperative, involved, and interesting persons before they became screen dependent. For these families, a hands-off approach has worked just fine. To do otherwise would definitely take parents out of their comfort zones. Why start using parenting strategies that feel as though they do not belong in this century? We are past the dour severity and strict parenting methods of our parents' generation, aren't we?

We, the authors, challenge anyone to show us the hard data behind the contention that recreational screen media use provides any real developmental advantage. In truth, all it provides are "empty calories" when it comes to development and learning. We have noted in previous chapters that screen media use, especially gaming, *does not improve* a child's imagination, problem solving, reaction time, or social skills. Video games simply teach children through repetition and trial and error what moves to make so as to proceed forward in the game. It is all scripted. Too much gaming makes children dumb and dumber, not smart and smarter![116]

There are good reasons not to fault parents for promoting their children's game use. Typically, screen dependence *does* reduce the hassles they have with their children, similar to the use of pot or some other mind-altering drug. It makes children invisible. Seventeen-year-old boys no longer care about cars or building the fastest one on the road. Seventeen-year-old girls are less likely to get into trouble with bad boys coming to sneak them out at night. They can have virtual sex with their boyfriends, sexting them with erotic content using Snapchat that magically disappears ten seconds after viewing. Everything is cool, safe, and predictable. No hormone surges or impulsivity. And parents have the predictability in their lives that is so valued by their employers.

The problem is that the human nervous system requires challenge to grow. Children who compulsively use screen media may be passive and quiet most of the time. They leave their parents alone as long as they get their screen fix. But underneath the façade of their placid exteriors, ordinary, real-world encounters that should be happening for their children are not happening. People learn from both their mistakes and successes in the real world. Neither of these things is happening in the virtual world.

The powerful impact of media industry propaganda

It is difficult to talk about recreational screen dependence in children without getting labeled as a spoiler or doomsayer—a person who obviously does not understand that screen media use brings children so much joy that it is almost unpatriotic to suggest that it could also have toxic influences on them.

Digital media companies spend thousands or millions of dollars telling consumers that it is beneficial for children to get on screens early and use them frequently. It is reminiscent of the old television ad campaigns for cigarettes—marvelous mind manipulation suggesting that somehow cigarettes aren't all that bad and might even be *good* for you.

In a recent *Psychology Today* article, a proponent of the use of video games suggests that children live "gamefully," developing "power ups" to deal with hassles in life. She goes on to say that gameful actions create "a quick moment of pleasure, strength, courage, or connection." Directly contradicting the majority of research on the subject, the author claims the University of Pennsylvania conducted a randomized clinical study that concluded people who lived gamefully for thirty days experienced diminished symptoms of anxiety and depression. Also, participants were more optimistic, felt they had increased social support, and believed they had the capacity to attain their goals.

The author, a psychologist who herself plays a lot of video games, goes on to suggest that children can deal with difficult emotional problems by following the lessons about determination and optimism taught by video games. She concludes that the evidence supports that gaming is not only a source of entertainment, but it also is "a model for how we become the best version of ourselves."[117] The fact that this article would be accepted for publication by *Psychology Today,* an icon of popular journalism, shows how widely accepted the view is that recreational screen media use is good for you and the more you use it, the better off you will be.

We do not deny that there are many benefits to be gained by advances in screen media. In this book, we are simply addressing its impact on the day-to-day way people live together in families. We suggest that good things tend to have downsides, and the downside of digital media is its ability to retard, or even prevent, the emotional, social, and cognitive development of children who have an excessive and chronic pattern of use.

If children are going to be able to grow up with the capability to carry on the engineering and other specialized work involved in creating virtualization breakthroughs, they are going to have to be educated *today*. They are going to have to be able to solve problems, think critically, do the math, and live on their own. This means less time engaging in recreational screen media now and more time learning the important things in school, and in life.

Sooner or later reality brings denial to its knees

Parents who choose to challenge the power of the Internet for their children's sake will need a lot of strength, resolve, and pain tolerance. This challenge is a true rite of passage for them, a task that will require them to find strength in themselves that they did not know they possessed.

Awareness and clarity come from the parents' realization that a child is no longer *present* as a family member; he has dropped out. For many parents, it is the pain felt by the child's emotional absence from the family that brings about the wake-up call. They realize that his screen dependence and the systems the whole family has used to enable it, or cope with it, must be dealt with if they are going to get their child back.

Once a child's presence returns to the family space, a whole new array of options become available. But getting to that place may require that parents themselves first get out of their own comfort zones regarding conflict because the child may deliver an aggressive attack on their plans. She or he may yell, accuse them of things, try to guilt-trip them, or threaten them. Parents must assume the unflinching love of the samurai for his students and say, "My job is to teach you, and sometimes the lessons are hard, but if I do not teach you well, life may destroy you. That is why it is my job to teach you. That is the most compassionate thing for me to do in this situation."

Usually parents are brought to the point of letting go of denial by the natural escalation of a child's dependence on her or his screen pursuits. First, she or he begins failing in school and then loses interest in anything but playing online or getting lost in endless, useless social media pursuits. At the same time, the child becomes irritable and depressed.

At some point the psychic, emotional, and spiritual pain of all concerned parties becomes so intense that getting control over recreational screen media use becomes the first priority. It becomes abundantly clear that the screen dependence is depleting the energy in the family's life. With awareness and clarity comes action.

Building blocks of long-term success in managing recreational screen media use

Once parents have clarity, they are 90 percent of the way to their goal. At this time, a plan is needed. Chapter 10 is devoted to describing prework for the family's screen control plan, and Chapter 11 explores how to write and enforce the plan. Here are five parenting best practices for ensuring eventual success of the recreational screen control plan:

- First and foremost, parents own the presence of the problem and resolve to change the status quo.

- Second, decisions made by parents are *data based*. They do a survey of the child's recreational screen media time using the Screen Media Use Recording Form or another instrument to assess the amount of time involved in screen media use. And they use an assessment such as the BIGS-P to assess the severity of their child's screen dependency.

- Third, parents are willing to establish routines and structures to help their child deal with his temper, dyscontrol, and other emotional impacts of having his recreational screen access interrupted.

- Fourth, parents rely on *passive security* to enforce the plan; they understand screen, game, and Internet technology and have the will to shut down the router and confiscate the cell phones at a designated time.

- Finally, parents avoid arguments with the child and simply restate requirements. They do not yell, berate, or scold. They simply shut down access and keep it shut down.

The good news is that if parents can stick to their intentions and *work together* on the issue, there is a high probability that they will succeed. This success will involve a redefinition of the family's value structure as well as the creation of a screen control plan that is consistently enforced.[118]

A warning form the eerie wisdom of *Brave New World*

The Aldous Huxley classic *Brave New World,* written in 1938, is stunningly prophetic in its vision of the rise of corporations and their dominance in our lives today.[119] Huxley bypassed the obvious terror of his own day of Nazi Germany to focus on the future as it really would evolve.

Now, however, society is not kept in check by a minority of bureaucrats who use group orgies or soma (an intoxicating drug that was perceived to intoxicate and pacify the population). But the present day is similar to his futuristic society in that people embrace their oppression by their acceptance of screen and social media in their lives and their willing surrender of privacy. As in the case of *Brave New World,* things have become enormously superficial in the modern world, a few people control the many, and big corporations are greatly benefiting from the new status quo.

No one could beat the system in *Brave New World,* but parents still have a chance to turn things around, and this change will come as does any important change toward greater health and well-being in society—with awareness and action. First there must be acknowledgment of what is happening and the danger it poses to the health and development of children. Then parents must take action to ensure that the value they put on real human connection and dialogue occurs in the essential formative culture of their home. Parents must teach their children not to let any outside force, any corporation, any drug, or any lifestyle practice get in the way of the essential importance of their connection with each other and with the things that really matter in life.

CHAPTER 10

Implementing Screen Controls—Phase 1: Writing Your Family Values Statement and Behavior Standards

We have divided the explanation of how to implement family screen controls into two chapters, which cover Phase 1 and Phase 2. Phase 1 discusses how to create the fertile soil, the essential nurturing culture, for changing family screen media use habits through redefinition of your family's values. Phase 2 details the process for actually putting physical controls in place.

What you can imagine, you can achieve

Working as a psychotherapist comes with the privilege of watching people change themselves for the better as individuals and in their relationships and families. A person who is successful in reinventing her or his life has three factors in place:

1. The individual has the *capability* to make the change.

2. She or he has the *desire* to change

3. She or he has the ability to *imagine* the changed state. People achieve what they are able to perceive.

TO ACHIEVE ANYTHING, YOU MUST...

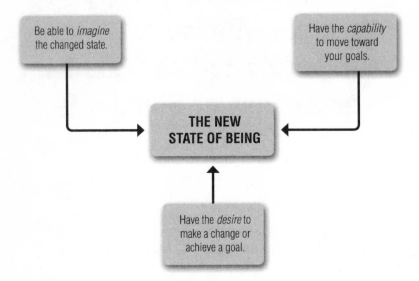

Looking at the change process for dysfunctional screen media use in terms of these three factors, it becomes evident that although parents may be capable of changing interaction patterns in the family and may actually strongly desire to change the situation, just *how* they make the specific change may be problematic because they cannot imagine the path to the changed state. The key is to create a clear visual picture of the how people in the family will interact after change and how the *values* will guide their interactions.

If your family values clarification process is successful, everyone in your family will experience a new vision of "us"—a new sense of congruity between espoused values and how people actually treat each other. Also, family members will start acting differently because they will have clarity on what beliefs, practices, and behaviors characterize your family and make it different from other families.

As the feeling of connection deepens between family members, the screen-dependent child's sense of incongruity, dissonance, and difference between his screen habits and his family's culture will become evident. Taking the time and putting in the effort to change your family's value system is worth it if you consider that your child's screen dependence will erode because it does not fit with the new family culture.

If you are to be successful in discontinuing your child's screen dependence, you will have to change the whole family system. Change will not occur unless the need for change is embraced in the hearts and minds of all family members, including the screen-dependent child; therefore, getting control of recreational screen media use will not come by parental command. It must occur within the context of a change in basic family values that are embraced by everyone. It must simply represent the logical extension of these values.

First acknowledge resistance to change

Change in your household's status quo may be covertly resisted by family members because of invisible forces at work. These invisible forces will vary depending on your family situation.

- One or both parents are deeply distracted by something. What distracts parents can vary from overwork to personal or emotional problems, such as underemployment or depression.

- This distraction has not resulted in the physical neglect of children but has resulted in their emotional neglect.

Parents may appear to be caring and in contact, but their minds are generally elsewhere, and issues with their children are typically more annoying than anything else.

- Communication between all family members has broken down, and family members demonstrate primitive communication strategies, such as blaming each other, placating each other, distracting each other, overanalyzing the situation, and doing nothing.

- Alliances have formed between parents and individual children, or, in some cases, antagonisms have formed that greatly structure any communication for the good or bad between these family members. A mother, for example, may become enmeshed with a child, believing everything he says, doing his bidding, and defending him from all criticism from the other parent and teachers. Or, a father may enter into an alliance with a son against the mother.

- Children have been allowed to take over the household. Anyone who has read *Lord of the Flies* knows how badly this can go![120] Whatever model of moral development one consults, all agree that children, up to a certain age, tend to be, for the large part, self-centered, impulsive, and lacking in understanding of how their behavior affects everyone else. Children should not be in charge for reasons particular to the survival of the family as a system. We have worked with many families in which the dominance of the children is painfully evident in every meeting. The children interrupt their parents, physically crowding them to prevent them from saying certain things or touching parents in the face. A particular child may act surly or telegraph a threat of a violent outburst with a dramatic pout.

These forces have staying power because they represent informal agreements that give predictability to the situation. After years of chaotic suffering, family members have achieved a pseudo-comfort zone for themselves. A kind of self-hypnosis occurs in which everyone accepts that "this is our family" or "this is just the way it is." Once this paradigm prevails, all attempts to change it are seen as "not us."

Screen media overuse is a symptom of lack of connection within the family. To heal this wound, it is necessary to first calibrate accepted norms of interaction in the family. Once this is done, anything that takes a family member out of the aura of the family—out of daily emotional connection with the family as a whole—will become immediately obvious. Thus, dissonance between the stated **belief system** of the family and the behavior of the screen-dependent child will exert a force for healing and reconciliation.

The train of thought here follows the importance of the great story for a child's identity development. It is just as important that *families* look at their *own* great story so as to consciously decide whether this is the story they want their children to live and take out into the world. Once acceptance of the need for change has occurred, the family is in position to formally renegotiate its identity—to literally rewrite its own great story, spelling out its vision of itself. A **values statement** lists values that collectively describe new ways for people to interact and new priorities to govern this interaction.

There is an additional benefit to this process: positive parental role modeling. Helping a screen-dependent child get better control of his screen dependence is not easy. His nervous system is pair locked with his practice, so cessation of his practice will cause him physical and emotional pain. To get through this misery, he must see his parents "walk their talk," and the first step is a courageous acceptance that things are not right and commitment to a new way of "being us" must occur.

Often parents seek the help of a family therapist, family clergy, or some other person who has a good understanding of healthy family dynamics and is not part of their immediate system. Sometimes it helps to have someone who does not have a stake in the fight come in and give people a different view of the situation. At the outset of this process, it is a good idea to ask one person to be the scribe, the recorder of the family's deliberations.

STEP 1: CONVENE ALL FAMILY MEMBERS TO WRITE A VALUES STATEMENT

You may want to use a statement such as the following for introducing the values clarification process to children and connecting it to the development of household screen controls. At an opportune time, perhaps when people are gathering together for dinner or participating in a family walk, a parent (Dad in this case) might say:

> Your mom and I were talking. We're concerned we are losing touch with you guys, so we want to actually have a couple of meetings to develop ways for us to be more in touch. To do this we want to get everyone together and write a statement of our family's values as well as some examples of what kinds of behavior express these values. This will be an opportunity for everyone to have his or her say.

> When we are done, we will have a specific description of how we want to treat each other and what our rules are for contributing to the family with regard to school, work, chores, and recreational screen media use (apart from homework). We single out screen media use because we feel that overuse of recreational screen media is damaging our family. We spend way too much time playing video games, texting, and drifting through YouTube, social media, and other screen enjoyments. We welcome your hearty participation in this process!

STEP 2: USE QUESTIONS TO IDENTIFY SHARED VALUES FOR THE FAMILY

At the appointed time, parents convene a family meeting. Having the meeting on the same day of the week at the same time for several weeks is easiest to remember. The task of your family is to form a consensus around a set of essential questions that, once answered, point to your family's desired self-identification within the family and between it and the larger community. These questions may include:

- If things are going the way you want them to go in our family, what are people doing on an average day? How are they communicating with each other, and what are they talking about?

- If a miracle happened overnight and all of our interaction in this family changed for the better, how would we be interacting the next day? What would people see in a movie made about our family?[121]

- How do you want us to be known? If others were talking about our family culture—the things we value—how would they describe us? As hard workers? As mutually supportive? As fun to be with *and* around? As people who value each other and go out of their way to stay in touch?

STEP 3: COMPILE ALL COMMENTS TO IDENTIFY ESSENTIAL FAMILY VALUES

You will be running this process, so in keeping with the current research, a values statement should describe key values of *strong families*.[122] The list *your* family comes up with should be written on poster-sized paper and displayed in a prominent place in your home. The following list contains some examples of family values statements.

- Our family is a community, and like any community, each member gets benefits and makes contributions. If a family member does something injurious, such as throw a temper tantrum that creates stress all around, there should be a giveback from this person to everyone else. Restitution occurs before reconciliation.

- In our family, we greatly value genuine connection between individuals: face-to-face, one-to-one, and one-to-all. We do not hide from each other in our work lives or rooms.

- In our family, we value school as an opportunity, imperfect as it is, for learning. We put a high priority on both studying and completing homework.

- Our highest priority is each other and our family. Nothing comes before that—not angry bosses who want parents to work until 9:00 p.m. every night and not pushy gamer friends who would try to bully us into betraying the values we hold dear in our family.

- In our family, as a group and individually, we value healthy living practices, which include getting enough sleep, eating well, moving and exercising, and maintaining a good balance of work and recreation.

In the values clarification process, everyone gets his or her say, and enough time is given to processing issues with a final agreement that no one seriously objects. For this reason, it may take quite a bit of time—weeks or months—for you to change the culture of your family. This involves *big listening*—listening without lecturing or trying to help your child see the error of his ways. Parents need to listen and make sure that all family members know that they have been heard and their voice is respected in the mix.

STEP 4: TRANSLATE YOUR FAMILY'S VALUES INTO BEHAVIOR STANDARDS THAT CAN BE MEASURED

Once your family's values are clarified, essential behaviors that express these values or violate them need to be described. Parents will be asking children to *stop* doing certain things and *start* doing other things. It is important that requirements are clear. The greatest stressor for a child is ambiguity about what his parents expect of him. If he has a strong character and is screen dependent, he will reflexively hone in on any weakness in his parents' position. Well-written behavior standards provide the structure that is necessary to ingrain new habits.

A good way to arrive at a set of behavior standards, which could be seen as the standards that will be enforced by your screen control plan, is to provide the following prompt to family members and ask each person to write a paragraph or two in response:

> Take a look at our family values statement and think about the day-to-day *behaviors* that express these values. For example, looking at the first value, the idea that our family is a community, think about things we do every day that express *respect* and *civility* or things that do not express these community values. Then write to these behaviors as standards, or rules of conduct, for us as individual family members.

To start this conversation, it may be helpful for you to provide multiple examples of behavior standards from your own experience. Once your family agrees on its set of standards, the list should be printed large enough so it can be easily read and posted within the family living area. Here are some examples that may be used as idea starters:

- We (children and teens) are proactive with regard to school. We work hard to stay organized, study the material, and do the homework. (Chronic issues with failing grades and lack of homework completion violate this standard.)

- While at school, we practice appropriate behavior toward all staff and our peers. (Arguing or insulting teachers, bus drivers, administrators, other staff, and peers violates this standard.)

- We do not insult each other using pejoratives or profanity. We speak respectfully to each other. (Swearing at parents and siblings violates this standard.)

- We use a calm and appropriate tone of voice and other nonverbal behaviors when we interact. (Whining or blaming when things don't go our way violates this standard.)

- We are never violent with each other and respect each other's psychological and physical space. (Pinching, hitting, or other physical abuse violates this standard.)

- We respect each other's privacy and need for rest and solitude. (Keeping parents up with loud music violates this standard.)

- We take responsibility for feeding ourselves (as age appropriate) or eating with family. (Asking for a separate dinner or disturbing people during dinner violates this standard.)

- We take responsibility (as age appropriate) for doing our own laundry, including gathering, washing, drying, folding, and putting away clothes. (Chronically leaving clothes scattered around violates this standard.)

HOW TO WRITE YOUR FAMILY VALUES STATEMENT

1. **Invite all family members to convene to write a statement of values.** In your invitation describe ground rules for the discussion—how you expect people to treat each other and what good listening behavior looks like.

2. **Once you are together, use questions to identify shared values for the family with examples:**

   a. "If things are going the way you want them to go in our family, what are people doing on an average day? How are they communicating with each other and what are they talking about?"

   b. "If a miracle happened overnight and all of our interaction in this family changed for the better, how would we be interacting the next day? What would people see in a movie made about our family?"

3. **Compile everyone's answers without censoring them. Then work down to five to seven succinct values statements, for example:**

   a. "In our family, we greatly value genuine connection between individuals, face-to-face, one-to-one, and one-to-all. We do not hide from each other in our work lives or rooms."

   b. "Our highest priority is each other and our family. Nothing comes before that. Not angry bosses who want parents to work until 9 p.m. every night. And not pushy gamer friends who would try to dragoon us into betraying the values we hold dear in our family."

4. **Translate the family's values into behavior standards that can be measured.** Take a look at your family values statement and think about the day-to-day behaviors that express these values. Then write to these behaviors as standards or rules of conduct for us as individual family members. Examples include:

   a. "We (children and teens) in the family may argue with each other or our parents, but once parents make a decision, we accept it." (Chronic arguing with parents or pestering violates this standard.)

   b. "We do not misrepresent the truth to each other. We own up to things when we have made mistakes." (Lying to parents or each other or the use of manipulative ploys violates this standard.)

   c. "We do not insult each other using pejoratives or profanity. We speak respectfully to each other." ("F-bombing" parents and siblings violates this standard.)

Observe a good communication process when conducting a family values discussion

Effective communication requires a good communication *process*. The values and behaviors a family identifies are the output, or *content,* of the communication. Content is the reason for communicating—the *why* the family is meeting part of the transaction. Process relates to the *how*—how the family speaks with each other in terms of the language that they use and their verbal and nonverbal behavior. A bad process can sabotage the best plans and intentions.

A good process in the family values clarification setting is shown in how you model appropriate behavior in a thoughtful and productive group discussion.

- **Use leveling techniques.** Speak from the "I," not "You," position. Describe behavior and avoid adjectives that put the other person down. Check for understanding by asking the other person to repeat and clarify if necessary. Specify your desired outcome clearly and behaviorally.

- **Give children safety to speak.** As in any group discussion of sensitive issues, people should be able to speak their mind without fear of retaliation. This does not mean that insulting, profane, or accusatory remarks are allowed. It means simply, "We are here to get to the truth and we will not hold anything you say against you. There will be no retaliation for speaking your mind. Please speak truthfully, free of the fear of being punished later."

- **Ensure that everyone is able to contribute to the discussion through the use of a talking stick.** It is very common in any discussion for certain members to dominate the topic and for other members to shy away from contributing because when they do, others speak over them. To prevent this from happening, appoint an object as a "talking stick" that can be passed around, giving the holder the right to speak his or her mind without interruption until the stick is passed to someone else.

When implementing the talking stick routine, it does not matter whether the object is a stick or roll of toilet paper or teddy bear. It is very important that parents be strong enough to repeatedly enforce the rule. Inevitably some individual family members will try to ignore it or talk over others in their enthusiasm to get their point across. It may take a while for everyone to get used to sharing the spotlight. Parents may feel frustration in enforcing the talking stick behavior, but it is worth the effort because once it is learned, the listening skills of family members are measurably improved.

The intangible result of the values clarification process will be a new feeling of unity and connection among your family members. The specific result, which will fold into your family's new screen control plan, will be a list of behavioral standards specific enough to enable ongoing enforcement of screen media use controls. Once you have defined your family's behavior standards, you are in a position to describe what constitutes a violation of a behavior standard and have the wherewithal to write a fair and enforceable rule.

We believe it is unwise to attempt to implement screen controls without specific descriptors of required behavior. Screen-dependent children are typically very good at eroding any attempt to control their behavior. Usually this is because the behavioral standard was not specific enough—there was too much wiggle room. Definition of behavior standards removes the fuzziness. So if an issue occurs, all you have to do is point to the poster on the wall where you have spelled out the behavior standards and ask your child simply, "What is the rule?" If your behavior standards are clearly defined, there will be no room for argument.

Strength in numbers: starting a family screen control group

One of the things we have noticed is that families with strong religious or cultural beliefs against recreational screen media use are the happiest. It does not matter what a family's religious persuasion is or what culture or country the family comes from. What matters is that the family is supported by other families in maintaining behavior within the home that is consistent with the religious or cultural values shared by the group, which seems to bring people together rather than push them away from each other. Not only is there a palpable feeling of love and support among these families, but also there are typically many successful students in their membership.

There is probably another reason why families who share religious or cultural values are much less distressed by screen dependence: strength in numbers. Parents in one family do not feel isolated in their screen control efforts. If control of recreational screen media use is challenged by one of their children, they can call another family for support. Many spiritual traditions teach us that it is easier to follow the tenets of a particular tradition if you are doing it side by side with others.

In this vein, we suggest that you discuss the possibility of creating a concerned parents' group with other parents in your neighborhood or with parents of children in the religious or cultural organizations that you belong to. What you may find is that you are not alone in the struggle you are going through as a result of recreational screen media overuse in your home. In fact, you will probably immediately hear other parents say something, such as "We are really glad you brought this up. Count us in! We thought that no one else had this problem."

Silver linings

An issue with screen dependence could be seen as the proverbial "tip of the iceberg" in a family—a symptom of conflict among family members whose interactions are guided by dysfunctional patterns. As the family rewrites its own great story and becomes clear on its values and goals and the everyday behaviors that spring from these values, the family *increases* its capability for long-lasting change. As family members sit down to contemplate and discuss what makes their family distinctive and what values they want to express as a group, change happens.

CHAPTER 11

Implementing Screen Controls—Phase 2: Executing and Enforcing Your Screen Control Plan

In Chapter 1, we suggested that the best place to start is by measuring the degree of the screen media use problem. This would be decided by analysis of the information gained from the Screen Media Use Recording Form as well as the BIGS-P. Once you have done a survey of the time your child actually spends using recreational screen media and an analysis of the degree of his dependency on screen media use, you are in a position to decide the degree of restriction you will require in your screen control plan, from **abstinence** to partial screen media use.

Factors that might predispose parents toward an abstinence plan

The term *abstinence* denotes the prohibition of any recreational screen media, including YouTube, games, cell phone applications, and social media. The only allowed recreational screen media would be television when the rest of the family is watching something and very limited use of texting (only in emergencies). Abstinence would be called for if parents judge a child to have severe screen dependence. During the acute phase of the child's screen withdrawal and for some time thereafter, abstinence would be the standard practice, with a change to a partial-use status once the child shows real progress in improving how he uses his time.

Here are some essential questions for you to consider when deciding between the need for abstinence and partial screen media use:

- Which of the three screen-dependent character styles does your child most resemble: the Gangster, the Golem, or the Charmer? We would suggest that the greater aggressive potential of the Gangster type of screen dependence weighs heavily toward the need to have stronger boundaries.

- Can your child be trusted to comply with the plan, or will she or he try to erode it over time? Initial acceptance with immediate argument is a strategy used by many adolescents. If there is going to be this type of gambit, it is best to start with abstinence.

- Are there psychiatric diagnoses in the picture? The presence of psychiatric diagnoses argues strongly for stricter boundaries around screen media use as straight-across symptom prevention. These symptoms may include an anxiety disorder that is related to too much social media use or an activated "chronically irritable" depression that is typically related to too much video gaming.[123]

- What is your child's motivation to go to school? If your child has no motivation, partial screen abstinence will do no good in getting her or him back. Parents may as well start with abstinence and build from the ground up.

Screen media use for school-related purposes would not be affected when using an abstinence or partial screen media use plan. Devices used for homework would be located in an area in the home that is reserved for homework and studying at designated times. This area would afford children some visual and sound privacy but would be subject to monitoring by parents.

Once media controls are introduced, a screen-dependent child will begin to go through central nervous system withdrawal symptoms. The period of time it takes a child to go through physical withdrawal from chronic screen media use varies. Generally it takes *most children ten days to two weeks* to pass through the acute phase marked by increased irritability, depressive affect, and heightened anxiety.[124] These effects should be anticipated by parents when implementing a screen control plan calling for abstinence. More about how to help the formerly screen-dependent child through withdrawal will be discussed in the next chapter.

To complete analysis of the issue and make a decision about the degree of control needed, you should supplement your own research using the BIGS-P and Screen Media Use Recording Form in consultation with your child's teachers and others, such as tutors, who observe him during the day. If he is chronically tired at school, he is probably staying up most nights and is sleep deprived. This would be an indication of more severe dependence. In less severe cases, a child may overuse screen media because, for whatever reason, he has a lot of downtime. This could be a result of poor social skills, lack of imagination about how to use his time, or the presence of a co-occurring psychiatric condition. Thus, some children use recreational screen media as a time *filler*. They can easily walk away from their screen media if something more interesting comes along.

Other children are hooked. If a parent attempts to control use, the encounter will be unpleasant. The child will fight to maintain access to the screen media. It is important to be clear on which of these two styles of use describe your child's issue with screen media *before* deciding on the severity of control measures.

FACTORS TO CONSIDER WHEN DECIDING BETWEEN <u>PARTIAL</u> RECREATIONAL SCREEN MEDIA USE AND <u>ABSTINENCE</u>*

PARTIAL screen media use may be indicated	ABSTINENCE may be indicated
• Compliant with parents' requests	• Aggressive in pursuit of screen interests
• Can be trusted; rarely resorts to guile or manipulation	• Not trustworthy
• No mood or conduct disorders are diagnosed	• Presence of the diagnosis of a mood disorder, conduct disorder, or oppositional defiance disorder
• Motivated to succeed at school	• Considers all of school to be "busy work"
• Gets enough sleep and does not try to subvert nighttime power-down	• Chronically tired during the day, very poor sleep habits
• Child is not overdependent on social media or obsessive about any screen media—generally accepts controls	• Screen media use is causing serious personality issues (social media shaming, online aggression)

*The term "abstinence" denotes the prohibition of any recreational screen media including YouTube, games, smartphone applications, and social media. The only allowed recreational media would be television when the rest of the family is watching and very limited use of texting (only in emergencies).

The question of rehab

In terms of the process of recovery from screen dependence, the abstinence phase would be the standard in rehabilitation facilities, also known as residential or inpatient treatment, for the duration of the child's stay (thirty to forty-five days). The aftercare phase, or outpatient care, that occurs when the child or young adult returns to home or college may be guided by either an abstinence or partial screen media use plan. For purposes of our discussion, we will consider the child's family home to be the return location for his recovery, post–inpatient treatment. What happens at home after he gets out is at least as important as what happened during his stay.

Our client analysis suggests that in order for a child to sustain good screen habits, the culture of his family, which includes the family's values, practices, and behavior norms, and the culture of his peer group must support his continued wise use. A good rehabilitation center can interrupt his screen dependence and help the child begin to build a new sense of identity. But once he is discharged, his screen media use habits will by and large be a product of how well his life outside the rehabilitation facility supports his progress.

Placing a child in a rehabilitation center should not be the first thing parents do, even if the issue is severe. If parents can hold the line for ten days to two weeks within the context of a family culture, renewed by the values clarification process described in the previous chapter, the child can pass through the acute phase at home.

What about texting controls?

Text messaging is fairly easy to control if the family has a group or family texting plan. Typically this involves parents contacting the company that the family uses for wireless phone and Internet access. Wireless providers, such as Verizon, T-Mobile, AT&T, and Sprint, have fields for "parental controls" on the main page of their websites.

Depending on the child's ability to moderate texting use, parents could decide to let their child be the judge of how much texting will happen. Or parents could assign a reasonable limit on a daily basis, such as "no more than twenty text messages a day." Once this decision is made, the phone vendor can apply the daily limit to the child's phone and lock it.

Children who text excessively typically do it more out of habit than out of necessity. If it is determined that your child is using a handheld device to access recreational screen media in addition to texting, you may choose to take away the Internet-capable phone and replace it with an older, basic phone with no Internet capability.

Parents make it easier on themselves if they are able to stand together on the idea that owning a cell phone is a privilege, not a right. However you decide to configure screen media use in your home, phones should be turned over to parents during homework time and before lights-out.

What about social media controls?

As discussed previously, screen dependence centered on social media could result in the development of a fairly severe social anxiety disorder and/or development of aggressive, bullying behavior in a child who would otherwise not show these behaviors. The damage done by social media dependence can be severe; children have committed suicide as a result of being shamed in social media.

Children who would not otherwise be members of a social network, such as those on the autism spectrum, are especially vulnerable to being damaged by online bullying. These children may have no friends, so the "friends" they make online are given the authority to judge them as worthy or unworthy human beings. Shame destroys people. If a child's screen dependence involves social media use, there is a high likelihood that she or he will be shamed, and some likelihood that the pain and self-recrimination that result could lead to self-destructive behavior.[125]

If there is evidence of the development of issues with anxiety and self-destructive behavior or online bullying as a result of social media use, consider implementation of an abstinence plan.

Implement an appropriate daily routine

At this point, several things have occurred that together form a strong foundation for execution of your screen control plan:

- You have written your family values statement.

- You have articulated the values identified as specific behavioral standards.

- You have measured the problem of your child's screen dependence using assessment tools and decided on the degree of recreational screen media use you will permit, ranging from abstinence to partial screen media use.

You are now in position to move to the implementation phase of the screen control plan by establishing *routines* for family members. Good family routines take the ambiguity out of the parents' home management task. Routines are simply standard operating procedures that clearly state what tasks are required of family members at any particular time. Within each child's routine, implicitly, will be the amount of screen media use that is permitted.

Routines should be written out clearly and posted in your child's room for daily reference. As a general rule, your child's school planner should be consulted on a daily basis to organize homework; for general study and reading time; and to complete other tasks and projects related to school. Once the work is done, it is a good idea to have your child make note of completed tasks in the planner. All completed work should be filed in your child's backpack for the next school day before any recreational screen media access is permitted. Again, phones should be turned off and given to you during homework and studying time.

When getting screen overuse issues under control, routines are especially important because they prevent a child from making screen media use the central and only priority in his daily life. As is the case for behavior standards, when a child argues for more screen time, all a parent has to do is point to the posted routines chart and ask the child, "What is on your schedule right now?" A typical daily routine for a child may include

- the time that he or she gets up in the morning;
- the approximate time for preparing to go to work or school, including breakfast and departure times;
- the approximate times when the child, siblings, and parents return home;
- the days and times when participation in sports occurs;
- the amount of after-school free time allowed;
- the time when each child in the family is to start on homework and studying;
- dinnertime and whether the child is expected to be present for dinner;
- the time when screen media use will no longer be permitted, if it is permitted;
- the time when all digital devices will be gathered and secured for the night;
- the time when lights-out will occur each evening.

A child's daily routine should specify how homework will be managed, either with close supervision or using a consulting approach in which parents do not review homework completion but make themselves available if children have questions. If a tutor is involved with the child, requirements for her or his compliance with the tutor's recommendations and homework assignments are stated.

It is important to create your child's daily routine with *her or his input*. Your child needs to feel like part of the family team before she or he will accept imposition of rules or routines. Behavior will not change if your child does not feel that she or he has been consulted in the development of the rules.

A brief introduction to level systems

The implementation of a screen control plan will involve the polite but sure enforcement of a daily routine for everyone including the screen-dependent child. The child may quickly accept any routine that eventually allows screen media use, but given that he has screen dependence, it is highly likely he will quickly forget to comply with the prescribed routine. For this reason, it is important for parents to make a decision as to whether they need to simply state, clarify, and post the new daily routine and the behavior standards that support it, or they need to enforce it using a *level system*. Parents have to determine whether they simply want to keep an informal record of compliance (this would probably suffice to help a child with mild screen dependence) or use a level system, a more institutional-like approach.[126]

A level system is a method used for enforcing behavior standards that records a child's compliance with behavior standards, along with clearly defined consequences for violating them. It is a *dynamic system* in that behavior standards may change depending on circumstances. One benefit of this kind of system is that it gives a child clear feedback on how well he is doing, along with a clear reward for following behavior standards.

Level systems should be written in clear, simple language. Typically a child's level is decided weekly, or every two weeks, on an assigned day. Depending on the child's success in complying with behavior standards, his or her level may increase (yielding more privileges) or decrease (yielding fewer privileges). Once a level is decided, there is no arguing about it. One of the strong features of level systems is seen in the certainty that, "as night follows day," if a child does well he will soon experience more freedoms and more benefits from his participation in the family community.

Noncompliance with behavior standards is measured by the assignment of infraction points during the week. These points are tallied when parents sit down to review the child's level. The higher the number of infraction points assigned, the lower the level. Most level systems use four levels. The child begins on Level 1 and works his way up to Level 4 with good behavior.

Each level is defined by the activities it allows the child and the restrictions parents put on her or him. Parents can change a child's level between assigned review dates if the situation warrants this change. As a general rule, violation of any rule or behavior standard around screen media use should be considered an enhanced infraction and should immediately result in loss of a level.

A good family level system is set up in writing and has three basic parts. First, it lists examples of the child's progress. Second, it shows the defined activities of a particular level. Third, it shows the behavior standards that the child is striving to meet. These standards should be numbered for easy recordkeeping.

Tool to record behavioral events

You can use the Event Recording Form in Appendix 3 to record behavioral events that will result in your child either gaining or losing points toward his assigned level. Make sure to note when he has exceeded a behavioral standard (his behavior shows greater maturity and self-responsibility) as well as infractions of behavior standards.

LEVEL DESCRIPTION: RODNEY'S EXAMPLE

Let's take a look at Rodney, an adolescent boy with significant screen media use issues as well as problems with aggressive, controlling, and manipulative behavior toward others in his family. The following shows specific prohibited behaviors that can cause Rodney to lose one or more levels, along with the violated behavior standard.

BEHAVIOR STANDARD	BEHAVIOR VIOLATION
1. Accept and respect parents' authority.	Disobeying screen media use rules.
2. Be respectful in communications with Mom and Dad.	Arguing with parents.
3. Show compassion and love for each other. Take care of each other!	Doing something deliberately hurtful or dishonest that hurts another person.
4. Use appropriate language at all times.	Using the "F" word at home or school.
5. Be respectful of others' physical boundaries and observe a no-violence standard.	Using physical abuse (pinching, hitting, or other abusive action).
6. Use appropriate school behavior (as communicated to parents by assigned student counselor or teacher).	Behaving inappropriately at school (toward teachers, students, bus driver, etc.).
7. Be respectful at dinner with regard to food and conversation.	Demanding that parents fix a separate dinner.
8. Be responsible for taking care of yourself.	Leaving dirty laundry around and whining when told to do laundry.

The following are examples of an Event Recording Form for Rodney and the level system his family uses. His parents can refer to each behavior standard by number on the form for a particular week. One point is assigned for each infraction of a behavior standard, and the total is tallied on the day his level is reviewed.

DATE	BEHAVIOR DESCRIPTION	BEHAVIOR STANDARD NUMBER
Oct. 10	F-bombed parents after chore request	#4—lost a point
Oct. 12	Showed flexible thinking in accepting requirement to mow the lawn	#2—gained a point
Oct. 15	Without prompting, showed compassion for little sister and helped her through some distress	#3—gained a point
Oct. 16	Participated in discussion of texting limits and willingly agreed to new guidelines	#2—gained a point

LEVEL 1—WHEN *12 OR MORE* INFRACTION POINTS ACCRUE, THESE RESTRICTIONS APPLY:

- The door is removed from Rodney's bedroom, and all electronics are removed.

- Parents transport Rodney to after-school tutoring, monitor his behavior there, and pick him up at the end of the tutoring.

- No electronic devices (television, Internet, phone, MP3 player, and so on) are allowed in Rodney's possession or used during the week except for closely supervised use of a designated computer for homework and school coordination.

- Lights out at 9:00 p.m.

LEVEL 2—WHEN 6 TO 11 INFRACTION POINTS ACCRUE, THESE RESTRICTIONS APPLY:

- Parents transport Rodney to after-school activities and pick him up but do not monitor him while there.

- No electronic devices are allowed in Rodney's possession.
- Lights out at 9:30 p.m.

LEVEL 2—ALLOWED ACTIVITIES

- The door to his bedroom is reinstalled.
- One hour a day of supervised television time of a parent-approved program is allowed.

LEVEL 3—WHEN 4 TO 6 INFRACTION POINTS ACCRUE, THESE RESTRICTIONS APPLY:

- Lights-out time for Rodney is 10:00 p.m. from this point forward.
- Digital devices are not allowed in Rodney's bedroom at any time.

LEVEL 3—ALLOWED ACTIVITIES

- Digital devices are inventoried daily and allowed in Rodney's possession.
- One hour per day, seven days per week, of game console, computer, or television time is permitted.
- He may invite someone from school for dinner or another activity.

LEVEL 4—WHEN 0 TO 4 POINTS ACCRUE, PARTIAL SCREEN MEDIA USE MAY OCCUR, AS FOLLOWS:

- Rodney may choose to use specified recreational screen media one hour per day on school days and weekends.
- Rodney may text friends when not at school and for a specified time before the nightly device roundup. Thirty text encounters per day are allowed.

- He may invite someone for dinner or other activity if all work is done, including tutoring and laundry.

- He may spend a designated amount from his allowance on permitted purchases.

Managing the home environment: the nightly power-down

Once parents specify the time when screen media use is to cease, they are in a position to close down the family's use of digital devices. Given that most children need eight to twelve hours of sleep, it is not difficult to determine when a particular child should be off his device. At this time parents should collect all cell phones and Wi-Fi–capable computers and secure them for the evening. *This rule applies even if the screen control plan does not call for abstinence.*

All Wi-Fi devices should be disconnected at the appointed time. The simplest way to handle the Wi-Fi problem is to turn off the family router, unplug it, and store it with other digital devices for the night. Wi-Fi routers are set up to reconnect automatically (when booted again) after being powered down this way. Alternatively, the router could be turned off and secured behind a locked door. If parents choose not to physically secure the modem, they should password-protect access to it and then change the settings within the modem's control panel so that it powers itself off or closes certain ports to the Internet at a specified time each day. All modems contain documentation about how to change settings that either comes with the device or is readily available online with the search phrase "download manual [specify modem make and model]."

Parents should periodically monitor the home network to determine whether a child is catching a signal from a nearby router using a *contraband device*. If this is the case, this infraction of the routine should be sanctioned by assigning a point or points to the child's level system and taking away the device for safekeeping. Parents should make it their business to know which digital devices are operating in their households so that use may be monitored and terminated at the assigned hour.

Children and adolescents today are typically more savvy about the technology that runs their digital devices than are their parents. They have been exposed to it all their life, whereas parents may have come to it later in life and relate to it mainly in terms of email and other ordinary work-related applications. If you are going to be effective in supervising your children's screen media use, you need to have a rudimentary understanding of digital technology. Acquiring this understanding would begin by taking an inventory of all the digital devices in your home and then doing research online to gather information useful in accessing a particular device and monitoring its use.

The importance of parental example

Parents must set a good example with regard to late-night screen media use. If the children have to have everything powered down by 9:00 p.m. at the latest, so should parents unless there is some work requirement involved. Parents often underestimate the huge impact their behavior has as a role model, and it does push their children's behavior in certain predictable directions.

Children hate hypocrisy with a passion. It fuels a righteous anger that can become a real problem, and it undermines the *moral authority* of parents—children no longer see parents as having the *right* to tell them what to do. When this happens, children may become unmanageable and openly defiant of any attempt to control their behavior. Being a good role model makes everything easier.

Taking the road less traveled may be difficult at first

Many parents who have chosen to implement screen controls tell us that choosing to live a reality-based existence rather than a virtual existence has been a *lonely* experience. Once the decision is made to pull back from accustomed patterns of screen media use, many families experience a break in social contact with people they had considered to be friends beforehand. This type of behavior shouldn't be surprising. Contemporary habits around social and digital media are shaped by the technology industry. Billions of dollars have been spent to convince people that doing things the industry's way—buying its products and giving up personal privacy—is in people's *own* best interest.

When a family makes the decision to buck the tide—to take back their hearts, minds, and lives from screen media—they also opt out of the social mainstream. If all boys and girls talk about when they are together is Twitter, their favorite video game, or Snapchat gossip, it may be difficult to interact socially with the children and adults who do *not* do these activities.

But as the tide turns and more families come to recognize how far they have gone from the things that made life worth living, more friends will appear. More contact will become possible. And it will be the children of these families who emerge from high school truly ready for college. It will be these new rebels, the new outlier children who have the physical strength, cognitive skills, and onboard sense of values and personal identity, who will rise to positions of leadership and success in the twenty-first century.

CHAPTER 12

How to Help a Formerly Screen-Dependent Child Battle His Demons

Once there is a screen-management process in place and holding, attention must shift to helping the screen-dependent child deal with the inner turmoil he experiences when deprived of screen access.

Help during the cold turkey stage

Chronic screen media use, spanning months or years, changes the way the brain functions, essentially locking the child's entire nervous system into a permanent state of "fight-or-flight." The brain gets used to this state, and before things settle down, the screen-abstinent child may experience withdrawal symptoms.

Withdrawal is a pain syndrome that involves headache, body aches, nausea, and sleep difficulties. This state of malaise, nicknamed *cold turkey,* occurs in the withdrawal phase of all addictive states and relates to how the brain tries to re-establish homeostasis (return to the neurologic status quo before withdrawal) through pain.[127] These symptoms typically fade within a week or so for a screen-dependent child. The compulsive urge to access screen media may be markedly diminished after going cold turkey, but the habit of automatically orienting toward a computer or phone screen to deal with boredom and everyday stress may remain for months.

Secondary impacts of screen dependence

Positive change in the life of the screen-dependent child will likely be slowed by the force of his habits—how he *used to* spend his time, whom he *used to* hang out with, and what priority he *used to* put on school and play. He will need help establishing new habits, which will take a lot of repetition and resolve. He will have to be motivated. The priorities he sets for his life will have to be genuinely *his* priorities.

Putting limits on the child's screen media use forces him to revise his great story—his sense of self-identity—by requiring him to make new friends and wrap his identity around a new friendship network. This is not an easy task, but there may be a silver lining: Doing things differently may nudge him toward a *different perspective*. He may come to see that his friends do not do anything with their lives except play online, and they do not respect him for anything more than his gaming prowess. And he may discover that as soon as he stops being an online luminary, many of these friends disappear. Feelings of abandonment, hurt, and confusion, as well as anger directed at parents, may result as the child goes through this internal struggle.

The child's social pain may be compounded by academic regression; it is not unusual for gamer children in the eighth grade—when their weekly online gaming or social networking may exceed two hours per day—to have the skill and ability set of fourth or fifth graders. It is extremely embarrassing for the child to find himself at the very bottom of his class, and although he navigated his own way there, he will need help finding a way out.

When the child was screen dependent, his obnoxious behavior may have alienated his parents so much that they do not give him much emotional support when he needs it most—in the discontinuance phase. Serious damage is done if their attachment to him has *weakened*. Attachment is the endearing emotional bond between parent and child that is essential for the child's normal neurological development. If a rupture in attachment occurs, the child may experience delays in cognitive, social, and emotional development.[128]

New friends eventually come into the picture, but before this happens the child may experience clinical levels of anxiety and depression. In fact, during use *and* in the withdrawal phase, anxiety is expressed in reclusivity and social fear. This is why many parents recruit a psychiatrist to help with the implementation and maintenance phases of a screen control plan. A psychiatrist may suggest lifestyle changes for the formerly screen-dependent child, such as new sleep schedules, and may provide consultation for best practices in terms of diet and exercise. She or he may also prescribe antianxiety or antidepressant medication to help the child through the readjustment phase, with eventual discontinuance planned once mood and cognitive function stabilize.[129]

One ray of light in this scenario is that if the child does not have an inherited ADHD condition on board, she or he may quite quickly experience a turnaround in brain executive function. She or he will be able to remember things better, be more focused, be less distracted, and be markedly more self-organized.

Recovery begins with the child's perception of identity dissonance

In an interview between journalist Bill Moyers and the poet August Wilson, Wilson says at one point in the conversation, "When your spirit gets larger, your demons get smaller."[130] Wilson's words are powerfully true in terms of the theme of this book: Although parents do well to provide strong structures, values, and behavior standards in their homes around the issue of screen dependence, there is no way parents can browbeat their children out of screen dependence. Instead, what they need to do is make their children's worlds *bigger* and find ways for them to experience themselves as *origins* of their own behavior, not tools of the economic or social systems in which they live.

Recovery from screen dependence requires two things. First, the screen-dependent child must buy into a new way of looking at himself (no longer a gamer), and second, he must come to see how this old identity *clashes* with a new, more positive identity. To use the social science term, he needs to experience *dissonance* between these two identity states. Parents get on the side of recovery when they help their child gently, but surely, move through this new identity negotiation that will result in his discovery of new answers to the three essential questions: Who am I? Who are all these others? What are we doing together?

Parents and other professionals can guide this process somewhat if the child sees them as his *allies*. In fact, the struggle to restore normalcy to a child's life involves, first and foremost, going into *alliance* with him to help him turn his life around. This means that parents serve the child's recovery process when they *do not* browbeat him, criticize him, or give in to his entreaties or manipulations, yet hold firm while providing any and all support for his recovery.

Parents provide the best conditions for their child to produce good answers to these three essential questions when they *pay attention* to him. In so doing they are able to intuit his strengths, core challenges, core interests, and aspirations and relate this information back to their child in such a way that he can mentally rewrite his own great story. Recalling the discussion of great story, people use this type of narrative to hold their sense of self together and move them forward in life.[131] A meaningful great story builds a person's confidence, spirit, and capability. A destructive great story builds a sense of futility and meaninglessness. When parents reference a positive great story for their child, they say, in effect, "This is what makes your spirit great. That is what we have always known about you!"

Humans are all works-in-progress, so it is impossible to describe an end state in any child's personal identity. But we have observed that once parents are able to establish a new status quo in their family, and people are back in contact with each other, the process of helping their children get back on the track of normal identity development becomes easier and more intuitive. As parents start paying more attention to their children, children start listening to them more and start putting a greater value on what they say. When you go into the home of a family going through this change, you immediately sense greater warmth among family members.

Helping your child through the four stages of recovery from screen dependence

Once you have established physical control of screen media use, what should you do to help your screen-dependent child recover? What practices are associated with good outcomes? A good place to start this discussion is to return to the idea that terminating dependence involves creating dissonance between screen media overuse and your child's new sense of self. Instead of spending a lot of time going over the evils of screen media use, focus on your child's success in achieving his goals, subtly, never directly, comparing his new success with the old way of being.

This is not the traditional **twelve-step model** of addiction recovery. The Alcoholics Anonymous model of brokenness does not have a place here because we have seen in our clinical and teaching work that children do not change as a result of hearing what is wrong with them. They can and will make dramatic changes if they believe that change *is possible,* that it is just a matter of time, and that there is something better to live for than chronic screen media use. We have observed that children go through roughly four stages in the recovery process.[132]

FOUR STAGES IN RECOVERY FROM SCREEN DEPENDENCE

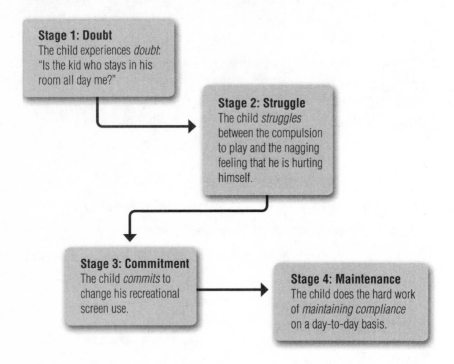

Stage 1: Doubt
The child experiences *doubt.* "Is the kid who stays in his room all day me?"

Stage 2: Struggle
The child *struggles* between the compulsion to play and the nagging feeling that he is hurting himself.

Stage 3: Commitment
The child *commits* to change his recreational screen use.

Stage 4: Maintenance
The child does the hard work of *maintaining compliance* on a day-to-day basis.

Let's look at some things you can say and do to encourage your child's movement in the healing process through these four stages.

STAGE 1: DOUBT

The doubt stage may actually occur *before* changing screen media use rules in the household. At Stage 1, parents nurture *dissonance* between the child's *potential* and his *behavior* through the use of gentle inquiries into his satisfaction with his own life, while at the same time giving him permission and encouragement to imagine a greater potential for himself. The child at Stage 1 may not consider himself screen dependent but may have misgivings and self-contempt for how compulsive his behavior has become. Parents do not scold. They simply seek permission to give information. The healing process in Stage 1 is shaped by comments such as these:

- "I've always seen you be a strong person with a lot of resolve to get past barriers to your success. I respect the way you are questioning the amount of time you spend online in terms of what you *really* want to do with your time."

- "Well, you seem a little tired and sad. If things were going the way you wanted them to, what would you be doing with your free time?"

- "I know you are working hard to stay in band at school, but they are threatening to kick you out because you are not turning in homework in your other classes. Need any help with organization or sleep habits? If so, look my way. And consider putting some time limits on your screen media use. I'd gladly tell you what has worked for me."

STAGE 2: STRUGGLE

At this stage, the child seesaws between wanting to change and wanting to use. This is a good time to draw out his personal values for himself or keynote values that have emerged from a family values clarification process. It is not as important to focus on his screen media use habits as it is to focus on his aspirations for himself or to give him new ways to imagine himself in the future.

- "Looks like you are struggling to find other things to do with your life besides going online. I know you can do this. I have always seen this resolve in you."

- "You have a powerful athletic intelligence and you are definitely a drama king! You could go into gymnastics or use it in acting school. Do you have any dreams about that?"

- "Your work in your ceramics class is incredible. I am really happy your teacher recognizes the artist in you. Are you taking that further, past high school?"

STAGE 3: COMMITMENT

If the child has negotiated withdrawal from screen dependence, he may arrive at a point where his *desire to change* overcomes his *impulse to use.* He is able to get through several days of greatly reduced access without experiencing high anxiety and voices a desire to stay the course. He is at a place where the cost of continual screen dependence is becoming painfully clear. At this juncture, parents serve the recovery process by helping the child set personal goals and challenging his intention to fulfill them.

- "I am so proud to see the *strength* in you around this issue. You are standing your ground!"

- "I am pleased with the choices that you are making and know it is not easy for you. You have the right stuff. You will get through this."

- "Okay. There are the bags under your eyes, and the yawn-o-meter just went off. Are you staying up texting? Do you need any help with that from us?"

STAGE 4: MAINTENANCE

The child enters the maintenance stage once his sense of commitment becomes "just the way things are." At this stage, a lot of the stress of dependence has left his life, and he now has energy to do positive things for himself that move him forward in his life. Now, the big challenge is to help him *remember* his commitment and express it in action. Sometimes it is difficult for impulsive, bright children to remember the path of their own healing.

- This is worth repeating: "I am pleased with the choices that you are making and know it is not easy for you. You have the right stuff to get through this in the long haul!"

- "You are incredible, but a freak to your friends, right? You actually prefer face time to texting! You go! So what do you say to your friends when they give you a hard time about texting?"

- "How do you remember to stay on your plan for your screen media use? What seems to be working for you?"

- "You know, Kid, I used to be a smoker, way, way back in my life. And it wasn't easy to quit. I have a sense of what you are going through. I am proud of you."

Using force field analysis to strengthen positive changes

Years of screen dependence creates substantial barriers to change simply because the screen-dependent child and his family have developed dysfunctional habits around use, homework, chores, and family communication. These habits have led to changes in the child's mood, social confidence, and capability to get things done at home and school. Maintaining any change in a family's communication patterns and culture requires *reducing* the forces that resist change and *strengthening* forces that are positive for change. This is known as a **force field analysis.**[133]

Forces that *resist* change are usually part of the social ecology of the child's life—the expectations, norms, and practices that he experiences in his home and with his peers. They are most often seen not as deliberate parenting strategies, but simply as aspects of "the way things are around here" and part of the parents' trance state, which may be especially difficult for parents to recognize. These forces include

- parents' collusion in allowing their child's unlimited screen media use because it gives *them* more time for work and other pastimes that they value;

- the weight of past parental disciplinary philosophy: "We don't want to be our children's overseers or prison guards. We want them to like us";

- the social isolation of the screen-dependent child along with his loss of social confidence and dependence on online friends who are also screen dependent;

- the child's dysfunctional physical hygiene—poor sleep, diet, and exercise habits;

- the weight of school failures and the low priority the child places on being successful at school, sometimes with the compliance and support of parents who blame their child's dismal GPA on the school's inability to teach him;

- the difficulty parents and children have in *imagining a future* for the child that is positive and reality centered rather than virtual and isolated.

If healthy screen media use habits are to be maintained, parents and children must enroll themselves in a new lifestyle that decreases the force of the bad habits noted previously and increases the forces *pushing for change*. Forces *strengthening* change include these:

- Parents, within the context of the family values clarification process, *model* their priorities: family first, work and other activities second. They do what they need to do to resist their employer's pressure to overwork and they turn to each other to renew their relationship. They put their first priority on spending time with each other and the children.

- Parents set the example by exercising self-control in their own impulses to overuse screen media. They put aside their cell phones and other media devices when they come home so as to make way for real communication with those they love.

- Parents make homework the first priority after school and devise routines to get it done and organized for turn-in. They may choose to be strict or casual, but do not let down their vigilance, and strive to consistently and accurately monitor ongoing progress at school through contact with teachers.

- Parents never criticize school staff in front of their children or make excuses for them. If they believe that the staff is delinquent in its responsibilities, they take immediate action to redress the issue with their child's building principal and use a collaborative and nonconfrontational approach in dealing with the staff member.

- Parents, within the context of the family values clarification process, embrace a change in their roles from the children's best friends to *protectors* of the children's best interests, even though this may cost them popularity points or incur their children's wrath.

- Parents and children work together to help restore the real, as opposed to virtual, social lives of their children. Parents help their children devise new friend opportunities through volunteerism, Boy or Girl Scouts, specialized clubs at school, athletics, or intellectual pursuits.

- Parents keep a log of their children's sleep, exercise, and dietary habits and institute new habits in sleep, diet, and exercise. Good sleep is the first priority, and parents set bedtime routines at home that encourage the return of good sleep.

- If necessary, the formerly screen-dependent child may be enrolled in one-to-one psychotherapy with a knowledgeable practitioner who can help him rebuild and regain social skills and mood control post–screen dependence. Our experience is that psychotherapy has minimal benefit if parents do not have a screen control plan in place. Screen-dependent children have a tendency to restart use and conceal it with some skill.

Physical activity is part of the healing process

As discussed earlier, the lack of physical activity may actually stunt muscle growth in adolescent males so that they look weak and much younger than their chronological age. This is a result of a lack of muscle challenge in the male body, which causes a drop in testosterone that retards development of muscle tissue.[134]

If physical inactivity is part of the damage done by screen media overuse, physical activity is part of the healing process. When you put together a screen control plan for your home, you should also envision activities for your children that are physical in nature and less likely to simply be gatherings of gamers talking about gaming. Trends in online games that get children out of the house to look for items should not count as physical activity because the children are still gaming. Physical activities might include

- being hired by a family member to do physical work;

- involvement in sports, ranging from the more conventional (the local softball team) to the less common (rock climbing, parkour, fencing, wrestling);

- dance;

- acting;

- martial arts;

- landscaping jobs or any job that requires body movement;

- participation in wilderness events, hiking, camping, facing a physical challenge, a teamwork project, or a "Tough Mudder" event;[135] or

- membership and daily use of a local health-and-fitness club.

Physical activity has been shown in research to reduce anxiety and depression and boost brain executive function. Essentially, physical activity brings your child back into his body. Getting physical, he opens up to the world and reduces the isolation caused by all the negative feelings and body states related to his screen dependence.

Recovery and mindfulness practices

One of the breakthrough therapeutic models to emerge from the late twentieth century is **dialectical behavioral therapy (DBT).** Created by Dr. Marsha Linehan at the University of Washington, DBT helps people strengthen themselves by practicing self-acceptance in the context of awareness and action for positive change.[136] DBT has been one of the few psychotherapeutic systems that has been validated as effective in the treatment of borderline personality disorder and in suicide prevention. DBT teaches the use of self-awareness to generate ways to self-soothe and deal with emotional distress that is not self-destructive. It puts a high value on a person becoming aware of the thoughts that precede some destructive behavior so as to enable him or her to choose new thinking patterns and new repertoires of behavior. It teaches skills in four domains that may be especially useful to children recovering from screen dependence:

- **Mindfulness:** how to pay attention to what is happening in one's life and make decisions thoughtfully, not impulsively

- **Distress tolerance:** how to tolerate pain that comes in one's life and learn ways to deal with it

- **Interpersonal effectiveness:** how to ask for what one wants and how to say "no" while maintaining self-respect and relationships with others

- **Emotion regulation:** how to notice one's emotional reaction to things and not be subject to habitual emotional reactions

DBT is a great model to use for structuring the help you provide to your child in the recovery phase. First, help your child *become aware* of the kinds of distress that might move him to access screen media to soothe himself. Author Dr. Sherry Turkle suggests that one necessary ingredient for the development of awareness is solitude, so helping your child first tolerate, then nurture, periods of solitude is very important.[137] Once limits are set up and accepted on the use of handheld devices, opportunities for good conversation and solitude become readily available.

Then help your child *imagine* different ways of *dealing with* these stressors in real time so he has a feeling of *control* and realizes he has done something meaningful to change the situation and does not need to soothe himself by accessing screen media. For example, teach him ways to calm anxiety through deep breathing. Or teach him assertiveness skills using the leveling approach so he can be more resourceful and successful in disagreements with friends. See Appendix 4 for a description of several techniques that are useful for reducing anxiety.

And help your child generate *imaginative alternatives* for self-soothing. Teach him ways to enjoy himself that build character, capability, spirit, and connection with people and the natural world.

As he progresses, continue to *keep the conversation open* about how he is doing and get into a coaching, not directing, role with him while maintaining firm boundaries on recreational screen media use. Pay attention to him and reinforce what new strengths and skills you observe in him. Make his ability to deal with the pain of withdrawal part of his great story.

The "no pain, no gain" rule applies here. In order for your child to open his mental tool kit—his imagination—he may need to experience some discomfort. If you can hold fast to boundaries you put on screen media use, eventually your child will have to create some novel, truly imaginative way to discharge the energy he is experiencing.

The fertile ground from which imagination and creativity grow

Mythologist Michael Meade says that the world children live in today gives them "no place to throw their imagination."[138] This phrase gets to the essence of the spiritual and emotional poisoning that occurs from screen media overuse by children: They stop *imagining* their own futures, have no interest in their own futures, and focus only on the images provided to them on screens. Unlike a child from an earlier generation, who may have felt frustrated and angry because his personal goals were blocked, the screen-dependent child stops having personal goals except with regard to screen media use.

Meade believes that modern culture leaves little room for personhood to emerge. Things are pretty tightly proscribed by the economic and cultural systems people live in. We build on Meade's work to suggest that screen dependence in children extends the reach of control of these forces into people's lives much earlier—not for any malevolent reason, but rather to make more money.

What can parents take away from this talk of huge market forces at work stealing their children's imagination? How does this knowledge help parents change the situation, if it can be changed? The answer is just this: if parents want their children to be imaginative people as they grow up, they are going to have to *let their children get bored.*

Boredom is the fertile ground from which imagination and creativity grow. Boredom is excitement unfulfilled. It is a pain state that is needed for people to get out of their comfort zones. For humans, it has worked this way for thousands of years. In fact, the greatest gift a parent can give a child who complains of boredom is to say, "Give me three things you could do about it right now." Playing online would *not* be one of the acceptable options.

Boredom is a signal that a child has energy for something but does not know what that something *is.* If the child's boredom is not remedied with the empty calories of screen media use, he will be forced to find something else to do with his energy.

The screen-dependent children we work with say that when they experience boredom they feel like they are stuck and staring at the ground in front of them. We hypothesize that these children have put themselves in a trance state of sorts that has shut down creative imagination and gone into replay of the mental message, "If only I could play my game or be online I would be happy. That is all I need. If my parents won't let me do that, there is nothing else I *can* do."

Sometimes "things to do" lists can be very useful for children and their parents as aids in breaking the child out from her or his "I'm bored" trance. The list provided in Appendix 5 will help you get the process going.

Take heart, parents! How to handle boredom is simply a script your child has learned along the way, and it can be unlearned and transformed.

Boredom

by Cynthia

One of the worst things a parent can hear is "I'm bored." Upon hearing this proclamation, many parents feel compelled to somehow cleanse the boredom from their child. With regard to this boredom statement, here are two ironic facts:

- **Fact 1:** There is nothing you can do to alleviate boredom in your child. Complaints of boredom from children with screen dependence typically mean nothing more than "I want screen time now! Nothing else will work!"

- **Fact 2:** Making this statement is a power play. Your child merely wants you to take the easy way out and let him play video games or use screen media. If you do not do his bidding, you will suffer the consequences.

I have witnessed screen-dependent children after the very first day of school say they were totally bored . . . with every class . . . with every teacher. I have also observed that students who are *not* screen dependent rarely complain that they are bored. They roll with the anxiety they feel and, listening to the inner voice of their imagination, discover new interests, new passions, and new directions.

CONCLUSION

You Are in Charge

We hope that this book has left you, a parent of a child growing up in the digital age, feeling emboldened to do what you need to do to restore a sense of care and connection within your family. Digital technology is here to stay and contributes positively to our society. But there is a dark side to technology, exploited largely for corporate profit by the recreational digital media industry—the abduction of children's minds and bodies. Your choice to engage the issue of screen dependence in your home makes you a soldier in an undeclared war that is raging quietly all over the wired world. The results of this conflict will decide who controls the spirits and minds of your children: those who love them or those who profit from them.

Digital media companies do not care if your child's identity is so stifled that he has no sense of himself and no intellectual or social confidence. They do not care that he has not developed a sense of empathy and connection, the fundamental building blocks of personal morality. They do not care that his cognitive development is so arrested by his screen obsession that he actually has lost IQ points. For the people who design, manufacture, and promulgate screen media, it is all about money.

The screen media industry has entranced us all, convincing parents that technology is so unimaginably all-present, so essential to everyone's life that it cannot be controlled, and parents can do nothing to protect themselves and their children from it. We disagree. Throughout the book we have discussed the experience of parents who have been jolted from this trance by the shock of dealing with the impact of their child's screen dependence, which was so destructive that it could no longer be ignored. We encourage you not to wait for this kind of painful wake-up call.

Here is the reality: The media industry cannot entrance you or your family unless you let them do so. You are in charge. You are, in fact, in a rare position to fight this battle and have a unique advantage. For the first eighteen years or so of your child's life, you have the opportunity to shape his development and the decisions he makes about what is important in his life. What he becomes later on will reflect his experience living with you as a child and adolescent.

What is at stake is your child's identity, the great story he writes about himself. This is an ongoing process shaped by the decisions he makes every day about what is important in life and who he is in the mix: hero, challenger, or dupe. Many voices and external forces influence the development of his identity. Your example and your family's value system in action are two of the most powerful influences on how he sees himself.

His peers and the messages they carry that are promulgated by purveyors of digital media also have a powerful influence on how he writes his great story. These messages are designed by the digital media industry to pace your child's developmental progress, providing virtual experiences of success and heroism within a game or other screen medium. This messaging is relentless and potentially destructive to the developmental process. He needs your protection from this influence until he is old enough to take a critical look at the situation himself.

We observe that when parents actually realize that they are in charge and decide to get better control of screen media use at home, there may be less of a fight to retain screen access than they previously imagined. Children typically accept family structures and values if it is clear that this is the order of the day. After all, they are children, not adults; they haven't been alive long enough to gain the wisdom to effectively run things themselves.

When we talk with screen-dependent children in our professional roles, we come away with the impression that they actually *want* stronger structures in their home and school lives. They do not really want to run the show. Doing so is as exhausting for them as it is for parents. What they want, typically, is parents' attention now—face-to-face, mind-to-mind, and heart-to-heart.

We have seen many parents take on the issue of screen dependence to eventually win back the hearts, minds, and spirits of their children. These parents do not try to deny the presence or power of the Internet or the benefits of technology. Neither do they spend a great deal of time talking about their own powerlessness in the face of the influence of digital media in their children's lives.

Empowered parents practice what they preach in terms of mindful use of screen media. They set the example and are clear on what is or is not in compliance with the family's behavior standards. They prize personal connection over virtual connection with others.

Parents serve their children by helping them tackle the joys and sorrows of being alive, encouraging them to commit to ideas and other people, and supporting them when they dare to love someone. A child's identity is built from this struggle. And parents do well by their children if they are able to demonstrate—through their own actions and personal examples—that as messy as life is, they value real life *and* their connection with their children over everything else. Moreover, parents love their children unconditionally and applaud them wholeheartedly when they actually take the risk to make a difference for the good in their own life and in the world.

APPENDIX 1

Screen Media Use Recording Form

Child's Name: _____

Evaluator: _____

Evaluation Date:

    Start: _____   End: _____

Directions: Use this form to assess the number of hours a particular child spends using recreational screen media. See Chapter 1 for a detailed description. You may wish to recreate this form using a spreadsheet program.

Screen Media Use Recording Form

DAY/TIME	SCHOOL RELATED?	MEDIA	HARDWARE	DURATION IN HOURS	HOURS OF SLEEP PREVIOUS NIGHT	GPA / MISC.

APPENDIX 2

The Brief Internet Game Screen - For Parents (BIGS-P)*

Answer these questions based on your son's or daughter's engagement with gaming over the last twelve months. Circle the appropriate descriptor of your child's screen-use behavior.

1. How often do you feel your son or daughter thinks about their current, previous, or next gaming activity?

    ☐ Never   ☐ Occasionally   ☐ Weekly
    ☐ Daily   ☐ Hourly   ☐ Always

2. Has your son or daughter become restless, irritable, angry, or anxious when unable to engage in gaming activities?

    ☐ Yes   ☐ No

3. Has their engagement with gaming activities increased in the past year?

   ☐ Yes   ☐ No

4. What is the average number of hours your son or daughter spends engaging in gaming activities each week?

   ☐ Less than 7 hours

   ☐ Between 8 and 14 hours

   ☐ Between 15 and 20 hours

   ☐ Between 21 and 30 hours

   ☐ Between 31 and 40 hours

   ☐ More than 40 hours

5. Has your son or daughter tried to reduce participation in game activities but found it too difficult, so they've continued engaging in gaming activities?

   ☐ Yes   ☐ No   ☐ Occasionally

6. Has your son or daughter lost interest in non-game related activities (e.g., sports, hobbies, family activities, etc.)?

   ☐ Yes   ☐ No

7. Has your son or daughter continued to engage in game activities despite knowing the problems they experience as a result of their use?

   ☐ Yes   ☐ No

8. Has your son or daughter deceived a family member, significant other, employer, or therapist regarding the amount of time spent engaging in gaming activities?

    ☐ Yes   ☐ No

9. Do you believe your son or daughter participates in gaming activities to feel better (e.g., reduce anxiety, loneliness, sadness, guilt, worry, etc.)?

    ☐ Yes   ☐ No

10. Has your son or daughter jeopardized or lost an academic or employment opportunity or significant relationship because of his or her engagement with gaming activities?

    ☐ Yes   ☐ No

11. Please select the option that best describes your son's or daughter's desire to change:

    ☐ They deny having any problems with gaming.

    ☐ Sometimes they acknowledge a problem with gaming.

    ☐ They have decided to engage in gaming activities less.

    ☐ They are already trying to engage in gaming activities less.

    ☐ They changed their engagement with gaming activities— they do not engage in gaming activities now or they engage significantly less than before.

Scoring

Please go over your responses and assign points as follows.

QUESTION 1

Never = 0 Occasionally = 5 Weekly = 10 Daily = 15 Hourly = 20
Always = 25

Points for question 1: _____

QUESTION 2

Yes = 10 No = 0

Points for question 2: _____

QUESTION 3

Yes = 10 No = 0

Points for question 3: _____

QUESTION 4

Less than 7 = 0
Between 8 and 14 = 5
Between 15 and 20 =10
Between 21 and 30 = 15
Between 31 and 40 = 20
More than 40 = 25

Points for question 4: _____

QUESTION 5

Yes = 10 No = 0 Occasionally = 10

Points for question 5: _____

QUESTION 6

Yes = 10 No = 0

Points for question 6: _____

QUESTION 7

Yes = 10 No =0

Points for question 7: _____

QUESTION 8

Yes = 10 No = 0

Points for question 8: _____

QUESTION 9

Yes = 10 No = 0

Points for question 9: _____

QUESTION 10

Yes = 10 No = 0

Points for question 10: _____

TOTAL SCORE

Add scores for Questions 1 through 10: _____

SCORE SEVERITY

35 or below: Minimal problematic Internet gaming

40–45: Mild problematic Internet gaming

50–75: Moderate problematic Internet gaming

80–105: Moderately severe Internet gaming

110–130: Severe Internet gaming

APPENDIX 3

Event Recording Form

Child's Name: _____

Evaluator: _____

Dates covered by this form:

Start Date: _____   End Date: _____

Directions: Use this form to record behavioral events that will result in a child either gaining or losing points toward his assigned level. See Chapter 11 for a detailed description. Make sure to note when he has *exceeded* a behavioral standard (his behavior shows greater maturity and self-responsibility) as well as infractions of behavioral standards. You may wish to recreate this form using a spreadsheet program.

DATE	BEHAVIOR DESCRIPTION	BEHAVIOR STANDARD NUMBER

APPENDIX 4

Anxiety Busters

If your child experiences anxiety, try one or more of these methods to help her or him alleviate symptoms. First practice the technique yourself to master it, then demonstrate it for your child.

BOTTLE BREATHING (ALSO KNOWN AS BOOK BREATHING)

Take a slow breath deep enough to push out your diaphragm. Imagine you are filling up the bottom of a wide-bottom bottle with the base of the bottle flat on your midriff. Breathe down deep. Hold your breath for a couple of counts and then release it slowly. Teach your child what deep breathing feels like by asking him to lay flat on his back and put a book over his stomach so that he is lifting it and lowering it a bit with each inhalation and exhalation.

FUTURE PACING

This technique is useful for dealing with time anxiety or performance anxiety. Simply imagine yourself "from above" going through the event as it would most likely happen and discern from that perspective whether there is something to be anxious about. Follow each such visualization with a deep breath in and out.

CALMING SELF-STATEMENTS

These statements are specifically used *during* moments of stress and anxiety. What you say to yourself depends on the situation. These are some examples:

- Relax; take several deep breaths; keep calm. This is really a minor matter that I can easily deal with if I keep my cool.
- Nobody here is trying to get me; keep a sense of humor.
- Relax. I'm in control. Take a slow, deep breath. Ah, good!
- Relax. I have studied for this test. I will rock it!

SUCCESSFUL EVENT RECALL

This method helps a child be more successful and less stressed by building her or his confidence and enlarging her or his self-concept. It involves simply the deliberate recall of situations in which the child functioned particularly well, felt at his or her best, and did a good job. It is effective to the degree to which the child is able to *vividly imagine* and *feel* a previous experience of success.

AFFIRMATIONS

Compose self-directed inner speech statements paired with visualizations that are repeated six times before getting out of bed in the morning and at different times throughout the day when extra confidence is needed to get through novel and anxiety-provoking tasks. It is important to visualize the event as though it has already occurred while repeating the affirmation to oneself. It is also important that the affirmation be noncomparative—that it affirms personal success, not superiority over others. The following are some examples:

- Every day, in every way, I am getting better and better.

- I move with confidence, skill, and power in everything that I do.

- I feel warm and loving toward myself, for I am a unique and precious being growing in wisdom and love.

There is some research to support the idea that inserting one's own name before using confidence-building, self-directed inner speech strengthens the method. These are some examples:

- OK, Larry, you can do this race. You can deal with the pace. Take a breath and get it done!

- Linda, this is not a big thing. It's just one of many math tests you will take this year. Just relax. Glide easily in your mind to the *A* that awaits you!

- Kevin, you are *rocking* this test!

Examples specific to recreational screen media use include the following:

- I welcome unstructured time as an opportunity to discover new ways to move forward toward the things I want in my life.

- I welcome the feeling of boredom as an opportunity to discover new things about myself and do things to make myself better and better every day.

Remember to visualize the image or feeling expressed in the affirmation. Repeat the phrase until you feel it "click"—you get a sense that the affirmation is good for you right now.

APPENDIX 5

Age-Appropriate Boredom Busters

ELEMENTARY SCHOOL

- Call a friend on the phone.
- Call your grandmother just for the fun of it.
- Invite a friend over to play a board game.
- Walk the dog or borrow a friend's dog and walk him.
- Ride your bike.
- Go to your local playground and join a game the kids are playing.
- Go sit in the backyard and make a list of the different animals and birds that you see.
- Read a book.
- Write to someone you love.
- Write a comic book.

- Research and find a board game you are good at and is fun. Then challenge your parents to play.

- Watch a funny movie (no more than one per week).

MIDDLE SCHOOL

- Lift weights, work out, stretch, or do martial arts.

- Go shoot some hoops by yourself or hit a tennis ball against a wall.

- Organize friends to shoot some hoops or play tennis.

- Cook a simple dinner for your family.

- Play with a chemistry set.

- Use a telescope at night and record what you see in a log.

- Take a friend to a movie.

- Give your pet a bath.

- Take a "penny hike" with friends—walk to the corner and flip a coin—heads you go right, tails you go left. See where it leads you.

- Write in your journal.

- Write a short story.

- Learn how to write a television script and write your own.

HIGH SCHOOL

- Cook a complex dinner for your family.

- Meditate for five minutes. Just sit, close your mouth and eyes, and breathe in and out through your nose. When thoughts come, imagine they blow out the window of your mind and return to focus on your breath.

- Go for a walk in the dark and train your eyes to see in the dark.

- Call someone for a juice bar or bakery shop date.

- Plan a day trip in the car to see something you have never seen before.

- Go mushrooming (in the fall, where they grow).

- Join a writer's group.

- Join a film discussion group.

- Go to a sports event or invite friends over to watch the game.

- Join a choir and learn how to sing.

- Join a robotics club.

- Get involved in theatre at school or in your local community.

- Develop a stand-up comic routine to amaze and amuse your friends.

- Get a job or volunteer at an organization in your community.

- If you have the talent, look for opportunities to be a model.

- Join a local "extras needed" actors' bulletin board and respond to casting calls for local productions.

- Join the police auxiliary.

- Organize a board game night with friends.

- Write a letter to someone who has made your life better and explain why.

- Do a "Tough Mudder"–type extreme obstacle course.

NOTES

1. Milton H. Erickson and Ernest L. Rossi, *Hypnotherapy: An Exploratory Casebook* (New York: Irvington Publishers, 1979). Erickson maintained that trance is a common, everyday occurrence. For example, when waiting for buses and trains, reading or listening, or even being involved in strenuous physical exercise, it's quite normal to become immersed in the activity and go into a trance state, removed from any other irrelevant stimuli.

2. American Psychiatric Association, "Internet Gaming Disorder, Proposed Criteria," in *Diagnostic and Statistical Manual of Mental Disorders, Fifth Edition* (Arlington, VA: American Psychiatric Association, 2013), 795–98.

3. John Bradshaw, *Healing the Shame that Binds You*, Health Communications, Inc., Deerfield Beach, Fla. 1991.

4. AAP Council on Communication and Media, "Children, Adolescents, and the Media," American Academy of Pediatrics, *Pediatrics* 132, no. 5 (2013): 958–61.

5. Ibid.

6. Andrew K. Przybylski, "Electronic Gaming and Psychosocial Adjustment," *Pediatrics* 134, no. 3 (2014): 716–22.

7. Tamar Lewin, "'Baby Einstein' Founder Goes to Court," *The New York Times* (January 12, 2010), http://nyti.ms/1G8y02D. *Baby Einstein* was started in 1996 by William Clark and his wife, Julie Aigner-Clark, who created an extensive line of videos with names like *Baby Van Gogh* and *Baby Mozart*, featuring music, puppets, and animals. The videos quickly caught on with parents, despite a 1999 recommendation by the American Academy of Pediatrics that children under the age of two should not watch television. In 2001 the Clarks sold their line of videos to Walt Disney Productions. In October 2010, under threat of a class-action lawsuit charging that *Baby Einstein* had been fraudulently marketed as educational, Disney offered refunds to those who had bought the DVDs.

8. *Second Life* is an online virtual world, developed by Linden Lab, based in San Francisco, and launched on June 23, 2003. By 2013 *Second Life* had approximately one million regular users, according to Linden Lab. In many ways, *Second Life* is similar to MMORPGs (massively multiplayer online role-playing games); however, Linden Lab is emphatic that their creation is not a game: "There is no manufactured conflict, no set objective." It is about building things, meeting people, and self-expression.

9. Josef Haik et al., "The Use of Video Capture Virtual Reality in Burn Rehabilitation: The Possibilities," *Journal of Burn Care & Research* 27, no. 2 (2006): 195–97.

10. Luke Gilman et al., "Tendon Rupture Associated with Excessive Smartphone Gaming," *JAMA Internal Medicine* 175, no. 6 (2015): 1048–49, doi:10.1001/jamainternmed.2015.0753.

11. Tom Loftus, "Virtual world teaches real-world skills," *NBC News* (February 25, 2005), http://www.nbcnews.com/id/7012645/#.VwQKUhMrJ9g.

12. Jonathan Vespa, Jamie M. Lewis, and Rose M. Krieder, "America's Families and Living Arrangements: 2012," United States Census Bureau (August 2013), https://www.census.gov/library/publications/2013/demo/p20-570.html.

13. Please see Appendix 1 for a larger version of this form.

14. reSTART Life, "The Brief Internet Game Screen - For Parents (BIGS-P)" (2015), https://www.surveymonkey.com/r/restart-BIGSP. Used with Permission. For further information, contact reSTART Life Organization Center, Fall City, WA, at https://www.netaddictionrecovery.com.

15. Section 504 of the Rehabilitation Act of 1973, 29 U.S.C. § 701 (Sept. 26, 1973). This law protects people with disabilities. The Individuals with Disabilities Education Act (IDEA) (Public Law No. 94–142) is a four-part piece of American legislation that ensures students with a disability are provided with free appropriate public education (FAPE) that is tailored to their individual needs. Overall, the goal of IDEA is to provide children with disabilities the same opportunity for education as those students who do not have a disability.

16. Lisa A. Jacobson et al., "Working Memory Influences Processing Speed and Reading Fluency in ADHD," *Child Neuropsychology* 17, no. 3 (2011): 209–224, doi:10.1080/09297049.2010.532204.

17. reSTART Life, "The Brief Internet Game Screen - For Parents (BIGS-P)."

18. American Psychiatric Association, "Internet Gaming Disorder, Proposed Criteria," 795–98.

19. Ibid.

20. Angie S. Page et al., "Children's Screen Viewing Is Related to Psychological Difficulties Irrespective of Physical Activity," *Pediatrics* 126, no. 5 (November 2010): 1011–17, doi:10.1542/peds.2010-1154.

21. Bradshaw, *Healing the Shame That Binds You*, 98.

22. Lev Grossman, "The Candy-Colored Ninja Doodle Angry Flappy Baby," *Time* 185, no. 23 (2015): 52–57; Joseph Kim, "The Compulsion Loop Explained," *Gamasutra* (March 23, 2014), http://www.gamasutra.com/blogs/JosephKim/20140323/213728/The_Compulsion_Loop_Explained.php.

23. Federal Cigarette Labeling and Advertising Act of 1966, 15 U.S.C. §§ 1331–40.

24. National Institute on Alcohol Abuse and Alcoholism, "Age of drinking onset predicts alcohol abuse and dependence," *NIH News* (January 14, 1998), http://www.niaaa.nih.gov/news-events/news-releases/age-drinking-onset-predicts-future-alcohol-abuse-and-dependence. People who begin drinking before age fifteen are four times more likely to develop alcohol dependence at some time in their lives compared with those who have their first drink at age twenty or older. Early intervention is an important deterrent to development of alcoholism later in life.

25. Cynthia M. Geppert, "Restoration," *Psychiatric Times* (July 1, 2006), http://www.psychiatrictimes.com/articles/restoration/page/0/1.

26. Robert M. Post, "Kindling and sensitization as models for affective episode recurrence, cyclicity, and tolerance phenomena," *Neuroscience and Biobehavioral Reviews* 31, no. 6 (2007): 858–73, doi:10.1016/j.neubiorev.2007.04.003.

27. Grossman, "The Candy-Colored Ninja Doodle Angry Flappy Baby," 52–57.

28. Erica Goode, "The Heavy Cost of Chronic Stress," *The New York Times* (December 17, 2007), http://www.nytimes.com/2002/12/17/science/the-heavy-cost-of-chronic-stress.html.

29. Hilarie Cash and Kim McDaniel, *Video Games & Your Kids: How Parents Stay in Control* (Enumclaw, WA: Issues Press, 2008).

30. Mary G. Burke, "The Impact of Screen Media on Children: An Environmental Health Perspective," *Psychiatric Times* 27, no. 10 (2010), http://www.psychiatrictimes.com/child-adolescent-psychiatry/impact-screen-media-children.

31. Norihito Oshima et al., "The Suicidal Feelings, Self-Injury, and Mobile Phone Use After Lights Out in Adolescents," *Journal of Pediatric Psychology* 37, no. 9 (2012): 1023–30. Web. doi:10.1093/jpepsy/jss072.

32. Stephani Sutherland, "Bright Screens Could Delay Bedtime," *Scientific American Mind* 23, no. 6 (2013): 13, http://www.scientificamerican.com/article/bright-screens-could-delay-bedtime/.

33. Mark W. Becker, Reem Alzahabi, and Christopher J. Hopwood, "Media Multitasking Is Associated with Symptoms of Depression and Social Anxiety," *Cyberpsychology, Behavior, and Social Networking* 16, no. 2 (2013): 132–35, doi:10.1089/cyber.2012.0291.

34. AAP Council on Communication and Media, "Children, Adolescents, and the Media," 958–61.

35. Aviel Goodman, "The Neurobiological Development of Addiction: An Overview," *Psychiatric Times* 26, no. 9 (2009), http://www.psychiatrictimes.com/addiction/neurobiological-development-addiction. Addictive disorders that are related to chronic stress tend to increase dendritic atrophy, accelerate neuronal degeneration, and subvert neuronal regeneration in the hippocampus and hippocampal and prefrontal cortex.

36. Ibid. Damage to the brain's memory structure, the hippocampus, has a direct impact on the ability to do homework.

37. Rachel E. Bender and Lauren B. Alloy, "Life Stress and Kindling in Bipolar Disorder: Review of the Evidence and Integration with Emerging Biopsychosocial Theories," *Clinical Psychology Review* 31, no. 3 (2011): 383–98, doi:10.1016/j.cpr.2011.01.004.

38. Hagop S. Akiskal, "Developmental Pathways to Bipolarity: Are Juvenile-Onset Depressions Pre-Bipolar?" *Journal of the American Academy of Child & Adolescent Psychiatry* 34, no. 6 (1995): 754–63, doi:10.1097/00004583-199506000-00016.

39. Amy Paturel, "Game Theory: How do video games affect the developing brains of children and teens?" *Neurology Now* 10, no. 3 (2014): 32–36, doi:10.1097/01.NNN.0000451325.82915.1d. Previous research showed that just ten to twenty minutes of violent gaming increased activity in the brain regions associated with arousal, anxiety, and emotional reaction, while simultaneously reducing activity in the frontal lobes associated with emotion regulation and executive control.

40. John McKinnon (Fitness Manager), from interview with Cynthia Johnson, Issaquah, WA (August 2015).

41. Hilarie Cash (founder of the reSTART Life Center), from interview with George Lynn (November 2013). A boy's sexual identity development may be influenced by what porn "teaches" him about the opposite sex; therefore, this is how he is supposed to treat the girls and women in his life. Eighty percent of boys who are diagnosed with a screen-media dependency show the presence of compulsive use of pornography; Philip Zimbardo and Nikita D. Coulombe, *Man (Dis)Connected: How Technology Has Sabotaged What It Means to Be Male* (London: Rider/Ebury, 2015).

42. Erin Coleman, "Nutrition and Short Stature," *SFGate*, accessed October 10, 2015, http://healthyeating.sfgate.com/nutrition-short-stature-11533.html.

43. Aldama Zigor, "Inside the Chinese Boot Camp Treating Internet Addiction," *The Telegraph* (January 17, 2015), http://www.telegraph.co.uk/news/health/11345412/Inside-the-Chinese-boot-camp-treating-Internet-addiction.html.

44. Erving Polster (Gestalt therapist and teacher), from interview with George Lynn, San Diego Institute of Gestalt, La Jolla, CA (March 1976).

45. Joanne L. Doherty and Michael J. Owen, "Genomic Insights into the Overlap between Psychiatric Disorders: Implications for Research and Clinical Practice," *Genome Medicine* 6, no. 29 (2014), doi:10.1186/gm546.

46. Michal Dubovický, "Neurobehavioral Manifestations of Developmental Impairment of the Brain," *Interdisciplinary Toxicology* 3, no. 2 (2010), doi: 10.2478/v10102-010-0012-4.

47. William Renthal and Eric Nestler, "Epigenetic Mechanisms in Drug Addiction," *Trends in Molecular Medicine* 14, no. 8 (2008): 341–50, doi:10.1016/j.molmed.2008.06.004.

48. AAP Council on Communication and Media, "Children, Adolescents, and the Media," 958–61.

49. Remarks from Demitri Papolos from his keynote presentation, "The Case of Lilly Abbott," at the Jean Paul Ohadi Center conference on pediatric bipolar disorder, Chicago, Illinois, 2000.

50. D. O. Hebb, *The Organization of Behavior: A Neuropsychological Theory* (New York: Wiley, 1949), 73.

51. Marilyn P. Dornbush and Sheryl K. Pruitt, *Teaching the Tiger: A Handbook for Individuals Involved in the Education of Students with Attention Deficit Disorders, Tourette Syndrome, or Obsessive-Compulsive Disorder* (Duarte, CA: Hope Press, 1995). Provides an easy-to-understand overview of the process and subtests in the educational assessment.

52. Daniel G. Amen, *Windows into the A.D.D. Mind: Understanding and Treating Attention Deficit Disorders in the Everyday Lives of Children, Adolescents and Adults* (Fairfield, CA: Mind Works, 1997).

53. Susanna N. Visser et al., "Trends in the Parent-Report of Health Care Provider-Diagnosed and Medicated Attention-Deficit/Hyperactivity Disorder: United States, 2003–2011," *Journal of the American Academy of Child & Adolescent Psychiatry* 53, no. 1 (2014): 34–46, doi:10.1016/j.jaac.2013.09.00.

54. American Psychiatric Association, *Diagnostic and Statistical Manual of Mental Disorders, Fifth Edition,* 168–71.

55. David Wechsler, "Wechsler Intelligence Scale for Children–Fourth Edition (WISC-IV)." The WISC-IV breaks out processing speed as a separate factor so as not to skew downward the IQ scores of ADHD children who tend to be slower mental processors.

56. American Psychiatric Association, *Diagnostic and Statistical Manual of Mental Disorders, Fifth Edition,* 155–88.

57. Gavin L. Brunsvold et al., "Comorbid Depression and ADHD in Children and Adolescents, *The Psychiatric Times* (September 1, 2008), http://www.psychiatrictimes.com/adhd/comorbid-depression-and-adhd-children-and-adolescents.

58. The Individuals with Disabilities Education Act (IDEA) (Public Law No. 94-142) provides the basis for state-funded home hospital services under its requirement for a free appropriate public education (FAPE) for students with disabilities.

59. Anderson Cooper, "Being 13," CNN, October 9, 2015.

60. American Psychiatric Association, *Diagnostic and Statistical Manual of Mental Disorders, Fifth Edition*, 222.

61. Ibid., 461.

62. Demitri Papolos and Janice Papolos, *The Bipolar Child: The Definitive and Reassuring Guide to Childhood's Most Misunderstood Disorder* (New York: Broadway Books, 2002).

63. Robert Post, "'Meeting Highlights: Early Recognition and Treatment of Schizophrenia and Bipolar Disorder in Children and Adolescents," *Bipolar Network News* 5, no. 2 (1999).

64. Ellen Frank et al., "Adjunctive psychotherapy for bipolar disorder: Effects of changing treatment modality," *Journal of Abnormal Psychology* 108, no. 4 (1999): 579–87.

65. Karen D. Wagner, "Diagnosis and Treatment of Major Depression and Bipolar Disorder in Children and Adolescents," from CME tape *Recent Breakthroughs in Child and Adolescent Psychiatry,* Irvine, CA (July 2000).

66. Donna Jackel, "Everything You Ever Wanted to Know About Bipolar Depression," *bp Magazine* (August 10, 2015), http://www.bphope.com/everything-you-ever-wanted-to-know-about-bipolar-depression.

67. George T. Lynn, *Survival Strategies for Parenting Children with Bipolar Disorder: Innovative Parenting and Counseling Techniques for Helping Children with Bipolar Disorder and the Conditions That May Occur with It* (London: Jessica Kingsley Publishers, 2000).

68. American Psychiatric Association, *Diagnostic and Statistical Manual of Mental Disorders, Fifth Edition*, 50–59.

69. George T. Lynn and Joanne Barrie Lynn, *The Asperger Plus Child: How to Identify and Help Children with Asperger Syndrome and Seven Common Co-existing Conditions* (Shawnee Mission, KS: Autism Asperger Publishing, 2006).

70. Simon Baron-Cohen, "Is Asperger Syndrome/High-Functioning Autism Necessarily a Disability?" *Development and Psychopathology* 12, no. 3 (2000): 489–500, doi:10.1017/S0954579400003126; Simon Baron-Cohen, *Mindblindness: An Essay on Autism and Theory of Mind* (Cambridge, MA: Bradford Books, 1995).

71. Helen Tager-Flusberg, "A Psychological Approach to Understanding the Social and Language Impairments in Autism," *International Review of Psychiatry* 11, no. 4 (1999): 325–34, doi:10.1080/09540269974203.

72. Dornbush and Pruitt, *Teaching the Tiger*, 173; American Psychiatric Association, *Diagnostic and Statistical Manual of Mental Disorders, Fifth Edition*, 31–41.

73. The Individuals with Disabilities Education Act (IDEA) (Public Law No. 94–142) provides the basis for state-funded home hospital services under its requirement for a free appropriate public education (FAPE) for students with disabilities.

74. Lewin, "'Baby Einstein' Founder Goes to Court."

75. James E. Marcia, "The Ego Identity Status Approach to Ego Identity," in *Ego Identity: A Handbook for Psychosocial Research* (New York: Springer, 1993), 3–21, doi:10.1007/978-1-4613-8330-7_1.

76. Jean Houston, *A Mythic Life: Learning to Live Our Greater Story* (San Francisco: HarperSanFrancisco, 1996).

77. Ralph Nader, *The Seventeen Traditions: Lessons from an American Childhood* (New York: HarperCollins, 2007).

78. Robert Kegan, *The Evolving Self: Problem and Process in Human Development* (Cambridge, MA: Harvard University Press, 1982). Many psychologists have written about identity formation, and there are multiple theories and constructs about the stages human beings go through from birth to adulthood and old age. Robert Kegan's construct is chosen here because it is the most accessible and least theoretical, and does suggest patterns seen in almost all theories of human development.

79. Marcia, "The Ego Identity Status Approach to Ego Identity," 3–21.

80. Douglas A. Gentile et al., "Pathological Video Game Use Among Youths: A Two-Year Longitudinal Study," *Pediatrics* 127, no. 2 (2011), doi:10.1542/peds.2010-1353.

81. AAP Council on Communication and Media, "Children, Adolescents, and the Media," 958–61. As noted in the Introduction, the American Academy of Pediatrics position on screen media for toddlers is that no child should be exposed to screen media before the age of two.

82. Thomas Lewis, Fari Amini, and Richard Lannon, *A General Theory of Love* (New York: Vintage Books, 2000).

83. Przybylski, "Electronic Gaming and Psychosocial Adjustment." This study suggests that children who use less than an hour a day of screen media have better psychosocial adjustment than those who play in excess of three hours.

84. Gentile et al., "Pathological Video Game Use Among Youths: A Two-Year Longitudinal Study."

85. Cooper, "Being 13." The show explores the development of other-centeredness in children who are dependent on social media for their sense of self-esteem.

86. Vincent Busch et al., "The Effects of Adolescent Health-Related Behavior on Academic Performance: A Systematic Review of the Longitudinal Evidence," *Review of Educational Research* 84, no. 2 (2014): 245–74, doi:10.3102/0034654313518441.

87. Marcia, "The Ego Identity Status Approach to Ego Identity," 3–21.

88. Lawrence Kohlberg, *The Philosophy of Moral Development: Moral Stages and the Idea of Justice* (San Francisco: Harper & Row, 1981).

89. *Unbroken* (New York: Universal Pictures International, 2014).

90. Rainer Maria Rilke, "The Man Watching," in *The Rag and Bone Shop of the Heart: A Poetry Anthology*, eds. Robert Bly, James Hillman, and Michael Meade (New York: HarperPerennial, 1992), 298.

91. Aric Sigman, "Virtually Addicted: Why General Practice Must Now Confront Screen Dependency," *British Journal of General Practice* 64, no. 629 (2014): 610–11, doi:10.3399/bjgp14X682597.

92. American Psychiatric Association, "Internet Gaming Disorder, Proposed Criteria," 795–98.

93. J. R. R. Tolkien and Douglas A. Anderson, *The Lord of the Rings* (Boston: Houghton Mifflin, 1994). Tolkien uses "Gollum" instead of "Golem" in his text.

94. Sherry Turkle, *Reclaiming Conversation: The Power of Talk in a Digital Age* (New York: Penguin Press, 2015).

95. Howard Gardner and Katie Davis, *The App Generation: How Today's Youth Navigate Identity, Intimacy, and Imagination in a Digital World* (New Haven, CT: Yale University Press, 2014).

96. Ray Williams, "How Facebook Can Amplify Low Self-Esteem/ Narcissism/Anxiety," *Psychology Today* (May 20, 2014), https:// www.psychologytoday.com/blog/wired-success/201405/how- facebook-can-amplify-low-self-esteemnarcissismanxiety; Cooper, "Being 13."

97. Turkle, *Reclaiming Conversation*, 11.

98. Frank et al., "Adjunctive psychotherapy for bipolar disorder: Effects of changing treatment modality," 579–87.

99. The Individuals with Disabilities Education Act (IDEA) (Public Law No. 94-142) is the root law for all special education services in the United States.

100. Jennifer Falbe et al., "Sleep Duration, Restfulness, and Screens in the Sleep Environment," *Pediatrics* 135, no. 2 (2015), doi:10.1542/peds.2014-2306.

101. Burke, "The Impact of Screen Media on Children: An Environmental Health Perspective."

102. Turkle, *Reclaiming Conversation*.

103. This meeting occurred for parents of students in a degree- granting program that author Cynthia Johnson founded at Bellevue Community College (now Bellevue College) in Bellevue, WA, called "The Venture Program." Venture was the first program in the United States to award a college degree to students with the learning disabilities described here.

104. Virginia Satir, *Peoplemaking* (Palo Alto, CA: Science and Behavior, 1972).

105. Helen McQuillan and Brian O'Neill, "Gender Differences in Children's Internet Use," *Journal of Children and Media* 3, no. 4 (2009): 366–78, doi:10.1080/17482790903233408.

106. Andrew Moravcsik, "Why I Put My Wife's Career First," *The Atlantic* (October 2015), http://www.theatlantic.com/magazine/archive/2015/10/why-i-put-my-wifes-career-first/403240/.

107. Vespa, Lewis, and Krieder, "America's Families and Living Arrangements: 2012."

108. Catherine Hill, "The Simple Truth About the Gender Pay Gap," American Association of University Women (Fall 2015), http://www.aauw.org/files/2015/09/The-Simple-Truth-Fall-2015.pdf.

109. Frank Pitman, "Fathers and Sons," *Psychology Today* (September 1993), https://www.psychologytoday.com/articles/200910/fathers-and-sons.

110. Michele Willens, "The Challenges and Rewards of Male-on-Male Friendship," *The Atlantic* (January 17, 2013), http://www.theatlantic.com/sexes/archive/2013/01/the-challenges-and-rewards-of-male-on-male-friendship/267284/.

111. Suze Orman, *The Money Book for the Young, Fabulous & Broke* (New York: Riverhead Books, 2007).

112. *Cool Hand Luke* (New York: Warner Bros., 1967).

113. Craig Jerald, "Keeping Kids in School: What Research Tells Us About Preventing Dropouts," *Center for Public Education* (April 5, 2007), http://www.centerforpubliceducation.org/Main-Menu/Staffingstudents/Keeping-kids-in-school-At-a-glance/Keeping-kids-in-school-Preventing-dropouts.html.

114. A primary virtualization application is *Second Life,* an online virtual world developed by Linden Lab, based in San Francisco, and launched on June 23, 2003. The app gives the user's avatar-type character the ability to be virtually involved in hundreds of different realistically drawn scenarios ranging from college classrooms to negotiating social contacts in a bar.

115. Michael Meade, *Fate and Destiny: The Two Agreements in Life* (Seattle: Mosaic Multicultural Foundation, 2007). Audio CD.

116. L. D. Rosen et al., "Media and Technology Use Predicts Ill-being among Children, Preteens and Teenagers Independent of the Negative Health Impacts of Exercise and Eating Habits," *Computers in Human Behavior* 35 (June 2014): 364–75, doi:10.1016/j.chb.2014.01.036.

117. Jane McGonigal, "It's Time to Think Like a Gamer," *Psychology Today* (August 28, 2015), https://www.psychologytoday.com/articles/201508/it-s-time-think-gamer.

118. Susan A. Carlson et al., "Influence of Limit-Setting and Participation in Physical Activity on Youth Screen Time," *Pediatrics* 126, no. 1 (2010): 89–96, doi:10.1542/peds.2009-3374.

119. Aldous Huxley, *Brave New World* (New York: Harper & Bros., 1946).

120. William Golding, *Lord of the Flies* (London: Faber and Faber, 1954).

121. Asking family members how things will look after they are changed evokes their imagination past all the complaints they have about what is going on right now. This question is similar to the "miracle question" used to keynote psychotherapy sessions with families and builds on the essential fact that change in psychotherapy does not come from recitation of failures, insults, and sorrows but from focus on strengths, resources, and possibilities in the situation.

122. George T. Lynn and Joanne Barrie Lynn, *Genius! Nurturing the Spirit of the Wild, Odd, and Oppositional Child* (London: Jessica Kingsley Publishers, 2006).

123. Oshima et al., "The Suicidal Feelings, Self-Injury, and Mobile Phone Use After Lights Out in Adolescents"; Becker, "Media Multitasking Is Associated with Symptoms of Depression and Social Anxiety."

124. Michela Romano et al., "Differential Psychological Impact of Internet Exposure on Internet Addicts," *PLoS ONE* 8, no. 2 (2013): e55162, doi:10.1371/journal.pone.0055162.

125. Micah O. Mazurek and Christopher R. Engelhardt, "Video Game Use in Boys with Autism Spectrum Disorder, ADHD, or Typical Development," *Pediatrics* 132, no. 2 (2013), doi:10.1542/peds.2012-3956.

126. Level systems are the standard process used for behavioral control of patients in inpatient psychiatric hospitals and some addiction rehabilitation centers.

127. Sigman, "Virtually Addicted: Why General Practice Must Now Confront Screen Dependency," 610–11.

128. Daniel J. Siegel, *The Developing Mind: How Relationships and the Brain Interact to Shape Who We Are* (New York: Guilford Press, 1999).

129. Psychiatrists prescribe antidepressant medication for their depressed parents and may supplement this treatment with addition of an antipsychotic medication. In screen-dependent children, depression is related to sleep deprivation, the toxic effects of chronic low-level brain stress caused by recreational media and video gaming, or the social stress related to excessive social media use. Once normal sleep cycles are restored, these potentially serious conditions may resolve and no longer require medication.

130. Jackson R. Bryer and Mary C. Hartig, *Conversations with August Wilson* (Jackson, MS: University Press of Mississippi, 2006).

131. Houston, *A Mythic Life.*

132. Richard Bostad and Margot Hamblett, "Transforming Recovery: NLP and Addiction," *Neurosemantics,* http://www. neurosemantics.com/transforming-recovery-nlp-and-addiction. This book's authors were inspired by this primary reference for modeling the recovery approach that shows best results working with children with screen dependencies. Psychotherapeutic methods derived from the neuro-linguistic programming (NLP) perspective provide tools that can be highly efficacious with this population.

133. Kurt Lewin, "Defining the 'Field at a Given Time,'" *Psychological Review* 50, no. 3 (1943): 292–310, doi:10.1037/ h0062738. Kurt Lewin gave us the Force Field Analysis technique in this seminal work on effecting change in organizations.

134. Refer to the Chapter 2 reference to John McKinnon's description of boys' "weakness syndrome" that is documented from observations of the physical underdevelopment of screen-dependent boys, adolescents, and young adults.

135. Tough Mudder is an endurance event series in which participants attempt ten- to twelve-mile-long (16–19 km) military-style obstacle courses. It tests mental as well as physical strength. The obstacles often play on common human fears, such as fire, water, electricity, and heights. The main principle of Tough Mudder revolves around teamwork. This can be a useful experience for formerly screen-dependent children in the recovery phase as it emphasizes re-establishment of connection with others in a setting involving extreme physical challenge. Both these conditions are typically absent in the gamer lifestyle in which mock challenge and mock teamwork replace the real thing.

136. Marsha M. Linehan et al., "Dialectical Behavior Therapy for Patients with Borderline Personality Disorder and Drug-Dependence," *American Journal on Addictions* 8, no. 4 (1999), 279–92, doi:10.1080/105504999305686.

137. Turkle, *Reclaiming Conversation*.

138. Meade, *Fate and Destiny: The Two Agreements in Life*.

KEY TERMS

504 Plan: Section 504 of the United States law titled the *Rehabilitation Act of 1973* that requires schools, employers, and other service providers to provide accommodations for people with disabilities.

AAP: The American Academy of Pediatrics.

AAP guidelines: Five recommendations from the AAP to parents for management of home screen media. Most recent version is 2013.

abstinence: The term denotes the prohibition of any recreational screen media including YouTube, games, cell phone applications, and social media. The only allowed recreational media would be television when the rest of the family is watching and very limited use of texting (only in emergencies).

addiction: The process through which the nervous system becomes psychologically and physically dependent on an experience or substance. Dependence can be measured both by accumulation of dopamine in the brain and by the degree of distress a person experiences when access to an addictive mechanism is blocked.

adrenaline: The hormone expressed by the adrenal glands during times of stress. Adrenaline starts the "fight-or-flight" response and kicks off the brain's use of dopamine to deal with a stressor. It may be experienced as pleasurable.

antisocial personality disorder: A diagnosis listed in the *DSM-5* to describe a person who evidences patterns of irresponsibility, lying, displacement of blame on others, and lack of empathy.

Asperger's syndrome (AS): Formerly considered "high-functioning" autism, AS is not included as a diagnosis in the *DSM-5*. People with AS have poor understanding of appropriate social behavior, poor understanding of the motivations of others, and poor social skills. These issues are often offset by brilliance in technology, mathematics, music, or any field that requires high pattern recognition.

attachment: A requirement for the attunement of a child and his mother on the level of their nervous systems. This attunement has been shown in studies to be a requirement for normal cognitive, social, and emotional development, especially with regard to capability to regulate emotions.

attention-deficit/hyperactivity disorder (ADHD): A diagnosis listed in the *DSM-5*. In functional terms, ADHD involves problems with short-term memory, attention, and task completion; difficulty doing things that are not intrinsically interesting; and moodiness.

autism spectrum disorder (ASD): A diagnosis listed in the *DSM-5*. ASD is a serious disorder of social communication. Autistic people cannot read others' facial expressions or nonverbal behavior. They do not understand others' intentions and motivations, and may not understand the *context* of social interaction—they tend to fixate on small details and be ignorant of what is happening around them socially and of appropriate behavior. These deficits may be countered by amazing talents in specialized areas, such as mathematics, science, technology, and the arts. Their strengths lie in pattern recognition, or the ability to connect the dots when focused on an area of interest.

avatar: A graphical representation of the user in an online media environment.

behavior standards: Written descriptions of specific behavior that are expected of all members of the family. A behavior standard proceeds from a value. If the value is "In this family we treat each other with respect," the behavior standard might be "We use respectful language even when we argue with each other."

belief system: A belief is something we assume to be true. A belief system is an interlocking set of beliefs that validate each other. Our beliefs structure our perception of what is happening around us. We literally see things as *we are*.

bipolar disorder: A diagnosis listed in the *DSM-5,* bipolar disorder is characterized by difficulty regulating good and bad moods, as well as controlling impulsivity and maintaining mental focus.

brain executive function: A term used to describe a set of skills required for successful functioning of children at home and school. These skills are impulse control, emotional control, flexible thinking, short-term memory, planning, task initiation, and self-organization.

Brief Internet Game Screen - For Parents (BIGS-P): An instrument developed by the reSTART Center located near Redmond, Washington, that is completed by parents to measure a child's screen dependence.

circadian rhythms: Physical, mental, and behavioral changes that follow a roughly twenty-four-hour cycle, responding primarily to light and darkness in a person's environment.

corticotropin-releasing factor (CRF): A neurotransmitter secreted by the hypothalamus in the brain's limbic system that triggers excitation of the nervous system to deal with a stressor. Too much CRF release can have a caustic effect on brain function, especially on memory and concentration.

DSM-5: *Diagnostic and Statistical Manual of Mental Disorders, Fifth Edition.*

dialectical behavioral therapy (DBT): A group-based psychotherapy approach devised by Dr. Marsha Linehan at the University of Washington that builds participant skills for dealing with emotional dysregulation, self-harm, and impulsivity.

dopamine: A neurotransmitter that plays a major role in reward-motivated behavior. Most types of reward increase the level of dopamine in the brain. Prolonged recreational screen media use causes a rise in the brain of levels of dopamine that are similar to those seen in opiate addictions.

educational assessment: A battery of tests given to a student to determine whether a learning disability is present. Usually includes an IQ test and analysis of the presence of issues with brain executive function and processing speed.

family values clarification process: A family meeting convened for the purpose of describing the set of values embraced by a particular family.

force field analysis: A method of problem analysis that begins with clear description of a desired changed state and then defines the forces that are pushing for the change and those that are resisting it. Change planning involves doing things to *strengthen* forces driving for change while *weakening* forces resisting it.

frontal cortex: The gray matter of the anterior part of the frontal lobe that is highly developed in humans and plays a role in the regulation of complex cognitive, emotional, and behavioral functioning.

game console: Hardware for playing certain video games including Xbox, PlayStation, and Nintendo Game Cube.

general adaptation syndrome (GAS): The "fight-or-flight" reflex triggered by stress that results in the activation of the adrenal gland, expression of adrenaline, and rapid cascade of events in the brain that prepare us to encounter or to avoid a stressor.

generalized anxiety disorder (GAD): A term listed in the *DSM-5* describing the presence of excessive worry that is difficult to control and may be associated with a set of physical and psychological symptoms. Physical symptoms include fatigue, restlessness, difficulty concentrating, irritability, muscle tension, and sleep disturbance. Psychological impacts may include school refusal, oppositionality, and avoidance of any task perceived as anxiety-provoking.

great story: Philosopher Dr. Jean Houston coined this term to describe the story we tell ourselves about who we are and what we are doing and supposed to be doing in life.

handheld device: Cell phones and body-worn devices such as watches, eyeglasses, and other dress accessories that enable connection with the Internet and screen media use.

hippocampus: The brain structure in the limbic system tasked for memory.

identity development: The maturation of a sense of separate self in people. It is the process through which they come to answer three important questions: Who am I? Who are all these others? What are we doing together?

Individualized Education Plan (IEP): A plan written by school staff, parents, and the student to describe the student's need for services, his or her eligibility for services, and how services will be delivered and measured. IEPs are established as a requirement of the Individuals with Disabilities Education Act (IDEA), a United States law that ensures students with a disability are provided with free appropriate public education (FAPE) in the least restrictive environment (LRE).

intermittent explosive disorder (IED): A term listed in the *DSM-5* to describe a behavior disorder characterized by brief episodes of disproportionate anger and aggression. Onset is in late childhood or adolescence. A child or adolescent with IED may impulsively explode into rage with little or no apparent provocation.

kindling effect: Research shows that brain cells that have been involved in an episode once are more likely to do so again, and more cells will become sensitized over time. In terms of depression, for example, if the first depressive episode is not treated, the second one will be worse. If the first manic episode in bipolar disorder is not treated, the second one will be worse.

learned helplessness: Inability to perform tasks caused by excessive caretaking by another person.

learning disability (LD): A neurocognitive impairment that interferes with learning in some specific way. Examples include dyslexia (reading impairment), dysgraphia (writing impairment), and nonverbal learning disability (NVLD, a condition in which a child retains information and learns from what he *hears,* not what he *sees*).

least restrictive environment (LRE): A provision of United States educational law that states the law's strong preference for educating students with disabilities in regular classes with appropriate aids and supports.

level system: A system that allocates privileges based on strict compliance with standards of behavior. A level system is built around the values articulated in a family's values clarification process.

leveling: A communication skill that involves getting "on the level," as an equal, with another, neither attempting to dominate nor giving in. Leveling behavior includes speaking from the "I," not "you," position, describing behavior you would like the other to change, and checking in frequently with the other to make sure you understand his or her perspective.

limbic resonance: The emotional energy that occurs between people who are in tune with each other and that enables deep connection and learning. It requires people to be in the physical presence of each other and involves unconscious synchronization of the limbic nervous system. The theory of limbic resonance was advanced by Thomas Lewis and others in the book *A General Theory of Love.*

massive multiplayer online role-playing game (MMORPG): The type of recreational screen media most likely to cause dependence, in which sometimes thousands of players do battle online representing themselves in different armies or clans.

meltdown: A temper tantrum usually enacted by a child who experiences severe frustration. Meltdown is different from *rage,* which has a much more powerful volume and is much more aggressive. A child having a meltdown is articulating, "I am beside myself with misery and do not know what to do!"

mindfulness: The practice of paying attention to our thoughts, feelings, and impulses so as to behave more *resourcefully* in our lives.

neurotransmitters: Endogenous chemicals that enable communication between brain neurons. Also known as chemical messengers.

planner: A personal organizer, schedule, and homework tracker.

reSTART Life: An Internet- and technology-addiction recovery program located near Redmond, Washington.

role-playing games (RPGs): Interactive online games in which the player assumes a particular personage or fictional character to play the game.

screen control plan: A written description of the rules and expectations governing the use of recreational screen media in the home.

screen dependence: A mental state characterized by excessive reliance on screen media use to the degree that a person experiences significant distress when deprived of access to favorite media.

screen media: A general term used to describe visual digital content created to educate or entertain users or to market goods to them.

Screen Media Use Recording Form: An instrument that provides a way to assess the number of hours a particular child spends using recreational screen media.

serotonin: A neurotransmitter involved in the regulation of mood, appetite, and sleep. Serotonin also has some cognitive functions, including memory and learning.

short-term memory: Also known as "ready memory," contains a limited amount of information for a very short period of time, from seconds to seven to ten minutes. It is primarily *acoustic*— consisting of words we say to ourselves.

social anxiety disorder: A type of anxiety disorder marked by avoidance of social situations and the presence of physical symptoms of anxiety in these situations.

social media: Computer-based tools that allow people to create, share, or exchange information, career interests, ideas, pictures, and videos in virtual communities and networks.

special education: The practice of educating students in a way that addresses their individual differences and needs. Common special needs include learning disabilities, communication disorders, emotional and behavioral disorders, physical disabilities, and developmental disabilities.

Supplemental Security Income (SSI): A United States government program that provides stipends to low-income people who are either aged sixty-five years or older, blind, or disabled.

trance: See *trance state.*

trance state: A psychological concept introduced by Dr. Milton Erickson to describe our patterned response to certain stimuli. Erickson maintained that trance is a common, everyday occurrence. We see things through our own belief structures, the invisible "bubble of perception" that surrounds us and filters all stimuli. We see things as *we* are, not as *they* are. In certain situations our reactions are automatic and predictable.

twelve-step model: A group-based approach to recovery from addiction promulgated by Alcoholics Anonymous that supports addicts in recovery through twelve stages, starting with admission of helplessness to an addiction and continuing through to carrying the message to others through example.

values statement: A step in the values clarification process in which family members brainstorm and identify what family interaction looks like in very specific terms when that interaction is guided by the family's chosen values.

weakness syndrome: A term coined by fitness expert John McKinnon to describe impairments in physical and psychological development in boys who are chronic screen media users. He believes lack of muscle challenge is the core cause of the syndrome.

yawn-o-meter: A term coined by Cynthia Johnson to describe the practice of gauging a screen-dependent child's need for sleep by counting the number of yawns that occur in a specific time interval.